MICHEL BUTOR

Jennifer Waelti-Walters

MICHEL BUTOR

A study of his view of the world
and a panorama of his work
1954-1974

SONO NIS PRESS
VICTORIA, BRITISH COLUMBIA

1977

Copyright © 1977 by Jennifer Waelti-Walters

Canadian Cataloguing in Publication Date

Waelti-Walters, Jennifer, 1942-
   Michel Butor

   Bibliography:
   Includes index.
   ISBN 0-919462-33-2

   1. Butor, Michel, 1926-   Criticism
   and interpretation.
   PQ2603.U73Z94   848'.9'1409   C77-002130-1

Published by
SONO NIS PRESS
Victoria, British Columbia

Designed and printed in Canada by
MORRISS PRINTING COMPANY LTD.
Victoria, British Columbia

TO

André Lequet and Jean-Pierre Mentha

FOR THEIR PATIENT HELP

Acknowledgements

This book has been published with the help of a grant from the Humanities Research Council of Canada, using funds provided by the Canada Council. The author wishes to express gratitude to the Canada Council also for research grants without which this book could not have been written.

Parts of chapters IV and VI have been published previously in papers in *PMLA* and *Diacritics* and a further section of IV was presented at a conference on Michel Butor at the University of New Mexico in Spring 1974 and has been published recently in *Contemporary Literature*.

Grateful acknowledgement is made to the following publishers for the reproduction of illustrations or for the permission to quote: Robert Altmann: *Querelle des Etats*; L'Arc: *Butor* No. 39; Editions de Minuit (*Ed. M.*): *Passage de Milan, L'Emploi du Temps, Répertoire I, II, III*; Editions du Seuil: *Musique en Jeu* No. 4; R. Barthes, *Littérature et discontinu*; Fata Morgana: *Tourmente, Les Sept femmes de Gilbert le Mauvais*; Editions Gallimard (*Ed. G.*): *Descriptions de San Marco, Dialogue avec 33 variations de Ludwig van Beethoven sur une valse de Diabelli, Histoire Extraordinaire, Illustrations I, II, Mobile, Portrait de l'artiste en jeune singe*, G. Charbonnier, *Entretiens avec Michel Butor*; B. Gheerbrant, La Hune: *Litanie d'eau*; Larousse: M. Butor et D. Hollier, *Rabelais*; Tel Quel: "Pérégrinations". And to the following artists for permission to reproduce their work: Camille Bryen: *Querelle des Etats*, Michel Butor: letters, games, *USA 76*, Jacques Hérold: *Tourmente, Le Grand Transparent*, Jiri Kolár: *Collage*, Gregory Masurovsky: *Portrait, Litanie d'eau*, Ania Staritsky: *Avertissement aux locataires indésirables*.

Finally I should like to thank Marina Gerwing for typing the manuscript so patiently and well, Caroline Monahan and Frank Waelti for toiling with me on the proofs and Index.   J. W-W.

Preface

This essay is an attempt to provide a synthesis of Butor's *Corpus* of writing rather than an analysis of every book. Butor's work appears to be a systematic exploration of one man's world in all its daily complexity, historic density and geographic possibility. The author is struggling to understand as much as he can of himself and his situation and each book is the record of further comprehension gained. I see the growing body of work as an initiation into the riches of our civilizations and of the human being in context. The levels of reference and resonance created by Butor are many, and multifaceted, and his writing reflects his quest in the intricacies and subtleties of technique, self-reflection and self consciousness.

In order to organize the mass of material, I have been obliged to draw divisions of a somewhat arbitrary nature but the reader must always bear in mind that the chapters of this study, should be superimposed and their contents interwoven once more before a full appreciation of Butor's work can be gained. He creates a multiplicity of coherences which are all mobile and in constant dialectic one with another within the body of work and each in turn reaches out beyond the books to the reality outside.

Butor provides an oscillatory action between imagination and reality, moving easily back and forth setting up, and interpreting fictional situations the better to help his reader deal with existant equivalents. The plan chosen by the author for the number of the periodical *L'Arc* (No. 39) devoted to his writing, provides, in fact, a schema of Butor's world and his way of perceiving it — hence I have adopted this same plan for my study because I feel that it emphasizes the major themes of Butor's work and enables all his books to be discussed from their most interesting angle with as little repetition as possible.

In *L'Arc* Butor places his material under the following heading: *Arts et Métiers, Sites, Musées, Spectacles, Livres*; the result is a discussion of craftsmanship first followed by a study of places which have a significance for the people in and around them. Sites are made by communal will and effort and are the result of a collective act of creativity. We shall see Butor show us how to notice and use all the complex information offered first by imaginary sites (the building in *Passage de Milan*, or Bleston) and then require us to use the knowledge gained in order to interpret real places such as Paris and Rome.

His presentation of museums is similar. Museums are collections of the work of individuals done in the past which, properly and significantly arranged, help us to understand the present and move on into the future. Sites have their mirror image in Spectacles which are also acts of collaborative creativity; Museums have their counterpart in books which tend to stress the individual and his opinions, so I have discussed Butor's criticism and attitudes to writing there. The order is significant also showing as it does man's acquisition of skills, his use of them collectively and individually, his knowledge of the past and the dynamic thrust it gives into a new creativity which has, again, collective and individual manifestations. Thus Butor's themes and forms to date can be encompassed and explored.

Around this schema taken from Butor himself, I have added two further chapters (to arrive at his favourite number — 7) just as he surrounds the sections of *L'Arc* with his own commentary. The opening chapter "Human Reflections" looks at *L'Arc*, Butor's and my relationship with it and also at the reflections created between Butor and his characters while the final one "Symbolic reflections" deals with other kinds of inter-relation those of systems used hermetically as ritual expression of a culture: alchemy, numbers and colours.

In this book, I hope to help the reader understand Butor's craft and the initiatory quest pursued in the various works in such a way that all future writing will be more immediately comprehensible and more rich. It is a study of a world view as drawn from the panorama of the first twenty years of Butor's writing.

Victoria 1976

Contents

List of Illustrations

Worksheets and Plates

8-9. *Querelle des Etats*, by Michel Butor and Camille Bryen, Robert Altmann, Brunidor (Vaduz) 1973, last triptych.

10. *Tourmente* No. 11, by Michel Butor and Jacques Hérold, Fata Morgana (Montpellier) 1968.

11. *Avertissement aux locataires indésirables*, by Michel Butor and Ania Staritsky, Georges Duchêne (Moulin de Larroque) 1974, detail.

12. *Bicentenaire kit: USA 76*, by Michel Butor and Jacques Monory, Ed. Philippe Lebaud (Paris) 1975.

13. Games invented by Michel Butor and Henri Pousseur to accompany the recorded version of *Votre Faust* BASF, Harmonia Mundi, 1973.

14-15. Letters from Michel Butor to J. Waelti-Walters.

16. *Le Grand Transparent* (1947) by Jacques Hérold, in *Petites liturgies intimes pour hâter l'avenement du Grand Transparent*, Ed. Galerie de Seine (Paris) 1972 (Sculpture 5 feet high).

CHAPTER I

Human Reflections

Michel Butor[1] has been publishing his writings consistently for the past twenty years. During this time he has produced some thirty major works of poetry, fiction and criticism, a considerable number of short pieces and various luxury editions created in collaboration with other artists. From these emerge a number of questions which have preoccupied Butor throughout his career: the position of man in the world today, as well as his own situation and his role as author. These produce sub-themes: the dichotomy between reality and dream, fact and imagination in understanding, the effects of time and space, and above all the problem of the expression of experience.

All of these will be studied during the course of this book which is itself built on a plan chosen by Butor for *L'Arc* No. 39.[2] This volume of the periodical being devoted to Butor, he was offered the chance to make of it what he would. The result was a schema of the Butorian universe that we shall see enlarged in his work as a whole.

The volume of *L'Arc* is divided into five chapters entitled "Arts et Métiers", "Sites", "Musées", "Spectacles" and "Livres". These are punctuated by five interventions by Butor himself, making ten sections in all. A dialogue is established immediately between the author, his work and his reader. The chapters are each made up of varied elements — lists, poems, short paragraphs, longer paragraphs, short and long articles — grouped around two illustrations which are antithetical, apart in time and space and yet each containing the essence of the subject of its chapter. Likewise the construction of the whole journal centres around the chapter "Musées".

The volume opens with a section on "Arts et Métiers" and closes with one on books. It is clear that for Butor craftsmanship and literature are linked and together envelop the world which finds its outlet through them alone. Next as we move towards the centre of the journal "Sites" is balanced by "Spectacles"; the first is concerned with the places which naturally provide situations within

I

which man acts out his drama, the second explores the way in which he chooses to give it created shape for and within his society. And in the middle of the work sits "Musées", from where is generated the power which stems from a knowledge of the past and can thus form the future. Here for Butor lies the development of man. Through his own skills he creates an environment, an art and tradition, rituals and drama, and the summation of all is his personal means of expression: literature.

The overall structure is balanced within the work. Near the beginning and end of each chapter is a list divided into ten points sometimes containing ten subdivisions of the tenth point. One of these lists offers real suggestions for study, the other imaginary works to be developed. They give the reader an opportunity to participate in Butor's world, to increase his understanding of his own, and to allow fantasy to play a role in his life. The chapters each also contain ten items, with the exception of the last one, "Livres", which has eight parts only. Its brevity is produced by the fact that Butor considers that the ninth part of it is *L'Arc* itself and the tenth the book the reader may himself write in the future. The journal turns in on itself and at the same time leads out into a boundless future.

L'Arc is a work of collaboration. People other than Butor wrote all the longest pieces. Authors from the past are quoted to give a sense of the historical density around us. Seemingly disparate subjects are juxtaposed to strike up the greatest resonance possible, and a balance is always maintained between reality and fantasy. Butor does not believe that any work can be anything but a collaboration and all his writing is devoted to making his reader aware of this. He says at the beginning of *L'Arc*

Il n'y a pas d'oeuvre individuelle. L'oeuvre d'un individu est une sorte de noeud qui se produit à l'intérieur d'un tissu culturel au sein duquel l'individu se trouve non pas plongé mais *apparu*. L'individu est, dès l'origine, un moment de ce tissu culturel. Aussi bien une oeuvre est-elle *toujours* une oeuvre collective.[3]

And here we have the key to the author's use of quotation, the pleasure he takes in working with other artists and the stimulus he tries to give his reader. Butor sees the world as a vast and ever-evolving pattern in which everyone plays his part. History as it is recorded in archaeological sites, old towns and buildings and individual works of art provides, if we are willing to study it carefully, a record of how the design grew to shape the situation we find ourselves in and which we are seeking to understand. Hence Butor's books described in the chapters "Sites" and "Musées" are his attempts to reveal the forces which inspire men to go on creating like works — these are dealt with in the chapters "Spectacles" and "Livres". They are explanations of the way the pattern is being continued around us. Every work is the product of a collaboration between the past and one or more modern artists. Butor's aim is that his readers should join him and his fellow creators in active participation, first by understanding their world and then by expressing themselves within it. *L'Arc* No. 39 is the manual of that aim.

The achievement of the ability to express oneself is not easy, however, for man must not only deal with the multitude of objects and happenings around him; he himself has many aspects which he must understand in order to profit from them to the full. The cover of *L'Arc* (plate 2, a collage by Jiri Kolár) shows Butor's face from many angles, enclosed within a circle (his world?) and surrounded by printed words. The result is an illustration of the author's basic problem; he must come to terms with himself as an individual and as a collaborator, for although he is alone within the circle, everywhere around him are the words by which other people describe their reactions to life and with which he must express himself. He cannot withdraw from the pattern. Butor is searching for a personal unity which must be part of a general harmony in which we must all participate, and to achieve this we must understand ourselves within our environment both as individuals and as groups. By charting his own explorations Butor is working to that end. He is offering a vision of the world as vast as that of Charles Fourier — we are part of a collective soul and must strive for collective understanding. It is for this reason perhaps that he wrote *La Rose des Vents*[4] which is essentially a collaboration in Fourier's universe, and hence an annexing of it to his own.

All Butor's chief preoccupations outlined and juxtaposed in *L'Arc* No. 39 can be found in his early poems and again in *Passage de Milan*. Thereafter they tend to reappear in some form in the three succeeding novels before being explored in quasi-isolation in a later work. Thus the themes branch in all directions, only to be pulled together at intervals the better to set off again. *Degrés* (1960), *Votre Faust* (1962), *Portrait de l'artiste en jeune singe* (1967), *Où** (1971) and *Les Sept Femmes de Gilbert le Mauvais*

---

* The title of Butor's book is *Où* and *Ou*. Due to the conservative rigidity of hot metal type a crossed out accent is impossible. We have therefore set it *Où* throughout and crave your indulgence.

(1972) seem to be the most important links in the network. If we trace some of the thematic developments through the work as a whole, we find that they move as follows:

The influence of Egypt — from *Passage de Milan* through *Le Génie du Lieu*, the North African character and the history lesson in *Degrés* to *Portrait de l'artiste en jeune singe*, *Où* and finally "Poème écrit en Egypte" republished in *Travaux d'approche*. That of USA — from *Degrés* to *Mobile*, *6 810 000 litres d'eau par seconde*, *Western Duo*, *Où* and *Quatre lettres écrites du Nouveau Mexique à Camille Bryen*. The problem of language — *Passage de Milan*, *L'Emploi du Temps*, *La Conversation*, *La Modification*, *Description de San Marco*, *Portrait*, *Rabelais*, and *Matière de Rêves*.

As more themes are studied, so the interaction of the individual works becomes more complex. *Passage de Milan* studies inter-relations within a building, *L'Emploi du Temps* in a town, *La Modification* between two cities, *Mobile* within a country, *Portrait* between several countries and historic periods, *Réseau Aérien* and *Où* all round the world. Meanwhile *Degrés* and *6 810 000 litres* return to restricted areas like those in the early work (a school and a tourist spot), and *Votre Faust* takes up the problem of man in a civilization which leads by another route to *Portrait* and *Où*. And in one of Butor's latest works, *Les Sept Femmes de Gilbert le Mauvais*, the relationship between one character (Proust's Marcel), a number of rooms and the social groups connected to them is discussed. The wheel has come full circle to the essays on Proust and on groups and rooms published in *Répertoire* and *Répertoire II* written ten and twenty years ago.

The appearance of Butor's books has changed greatly over the years; the early novels looked like traditional linear stories. *Degrés* was broken by a vast number of quotations and from then on the variation in form and typography has made each work look rather esoteric to the uninitiated. Certainly Butor requires effort of his reader, but he is careful to provide him with clues. Throughout his work he has shown the reader how to advance with him along the paths he explores.

He is searching for the words, objects, and places which are capable of throwing light upon everything around them, of giving reality a new significance and of forcing the author and reader into greater awareness of their situation.

Il faut se mettre à l'écoute de la réalité, il faut saisir le moment où la réalité commence à parler . . . il faut saisir les moments où, tiens, quel-

4

quechose que nous ne comprenions pas se met à se révéler à nous, quel-
quechose nous devient clair.[5]   (*Ed. G.*)

The sites Butor chooses to describe and the spectacles he creates or
selects are all representative of this attitude. Each one, as we shall
see in later chapters, is the expression in stone, in dance or literature
of a moment when reality revealed a part of itself to mankind. The
resultant work of art is the translation of what was understood into
human terms. Butor uses characters to express his experience in the
way that others would use stone or paint. Characters for him are
words of a higher degree. They are constructed for the purpose of
throwing light on a situation. Just as Kolár has shown Butor as a
man of many aspects, so Butor sees people as members of a number
of different groups, their lives as the meeting point of a number of
other lives and forces. *Passage de Milan* is the first illustration of
this. Each floor of the building contains a family of a different social
class: caretaker, priests, middle class, rich Jew, upper-middle class,
artist, servants and students. All are arranged so that their relations
to each other are inescapable. The rich and influential are deep in
the centre of the building and everything revolves around them. The
interest lies in the relations formed and reformed in this scheme of
Parisian society.

The characters in *Passage de Milan* and the succeeding works all
move in patterns which are used to two ends by the author. First he
describes them, juxtaposes his descriptions and allows the reader to
draw his own critical conclusions (Léon Delmont and the men
around him in the railway carriage are good examples of the possibilities offered by this method, as are the characters in *6 810 000
litres d'eau par seconde*). The technique invites reflection, clarifies
situations, comments on character and in no way refuses the complexity of each.

In *Passage de Milan*, for example, the layout of the book matches
that of the building it describes. Just as each floor of the building
is occupied by a different family, so each chapter of the book is concerned with a different hour of the night. Hence patterns of behaviour are set up which link time, place and people. In *L'Emploi
du Temps* these connections become forces which threaten to overwhelm Jacques Revel, and it is only because he draws on historical
comparison (the life of Theseus in the tapestries, the films of ancient
sites, Cain in the cathedral), on geographical orientation (the
Chinese restaurants, amusement parks, Old and New Cathedrals),
and on literary guidance (*Le Meurtre de Bleston*) that he is able to

survive with some sense of self. *La Modification* and *Degrés* follow similar lines, though *La Modification* is something of a controlled experiment. Delmont is spared the pressure of the advancing present by being inside the train for a set period, and so has an advantage over Vernier.

The heroes are all authors or have the intention of writing their experiences so that they reflect Butor's own struggle to express his situation. The division between experiencing man, man expressing his experience and the character through which he expresses this distinction is very important in Butor's work. So is the division between role and belief. Both are expressed by deliberately symbolic presentation, either by multiplication of meaning within a single character or by providing within a work multiple reflections of the hero.

An excellent example of the multiplication of meaning is the presentation of the Ralon family in *Passage de Milan*.[6] There are two priests who live with their mother, Virginie, and the German housekeeper Charlotte Tenant. These four, together with a cousin, Louis Lécuyer, form a many-faceted symbol of the Church of Rome, showing its beliefs, its position at the present time, the condition of its priesthood and its future.

Jean and Alexis Ralon, scholar and teacher, represent the dual role of the Catholic priesthood, yet it is obvious in the novel that there is no communication between them. Their only contact lies in the meals they eat together every day with their mother. Virginie, linked by her name to the concept of the Virgin Mary, is the symbol of Mother Church, while Charlotte Tenant is the every-day Christian. Virginie's dead husband, Augustin, is connected by his name to St. Augustin and the establishment of the modern church, but by the tale of his death he is inevitably transformed into a Christ figure, whose succession is taken by Louis Lécuyer (the squire) when the young man appears at the Ralon's door in the middle of the night with blood in the palms of his hands. Neither of the Ralon brothers sees him at that time, Alexis being busy with routine matters (the de Veres) and Jean with problems of faith (his dream), but Virginie is on the watch, as always, for new events within the Church.

Louis Lécuyer plays a major role in the Ralon symbol, and his actions during the course of the night can all be given a religious interpretation. Having seen the faults of the existing church (the Ralons), he is seeking a new creed which will incorporate the best of the old ideal (Virginie) separated from the broken-down priest-

6

hood (Jean and Alexis); Angèle is the new ideal. He thinks and dreams about her, but the modern world (in the shape of Henri Delétang) forces him to sacrifice her and become an outlaw because he has broken one of the basic laws of society. Like the Apostles of Christ, he is obliged to flee to a distant land for his beliefs. His dream is the symbol of the world destroying his new beliefs and hopes before they could mature fully.

Samuel Léonard, the Jew, can (ironically) be seen as the Good Samaritan helping the new prophet when his own people would not. Louis' beliefs are destroyed by the Modern World, and as a result of the destruction the Old World is able to gain a little more influence. Léonard, Jew and Egyptologist, is representative then of two forces older than the Christian Church. In sending Louis to Alexandria he is sending him along the path to loss of faith that has already been trodden by Jean Ralon. In Louis' dream the total decay of Angèle's face and the transformation of the head of the statue from that of the Virgin Mary to that of the Egyptian goddess Bast symbolize the change. Bast is often equated with Venus, so the transformation implies that Louis abandons religion for the world — a change which also provides a reason why it should be Louis on the shore calling Alexis when in the latter's dream his boat of faith falls to pieces. Samuel Léonard, with his relationship with Ahmed, his Egyptian houseboy, and his excessive love for Henriette, his "niece", would be the right person to push Louis down the slope of depravity. The situation indicates the resurgence of the pre-Christian religions after the fall of Louis, the last descendant of Augustin Ralon the Christ-figure.

In this description we have seen the symbolic resonance Butor builds into his characters. None of his people stand alone, isolated within one volume, created, defined and arrested. Butor's characters serve the same purpose as the books, works of art and buildings he mentions — they bear witness to the complexity of our situation, explain its intricacies to us and help us to grasp the pattern unfolding around us in all its richness. In *L'Emploi du Temps*, Burton and Jenkins are inseparable from Bleston, connected to it by detective stories, flies and the cathedrals. Léon Delmont by virtue of his name Leo, is an integral part of the history of Rome, through its connection with popes and emperors.

Usually the symbolic possibilities of a character are indicated by his name. We have seen the combination here of Virginie, Augustin, Jean, Alexis, Samuel, Angèle and Louis Lécuyer (the squire); such

7

an indicative choice can be found often throughout the novels, and always they tie the character to a function and/or context. For example, in *La Modification* the main characters are Léon Delmont, Henriette and Cécile. Delmont, in a crisis provoked by his increasing age, is torn between his allegiance to Henriette, his pious wife, in Paris and love for Cécile in Rome. The knowledge that there was a Pope Leo at all the important moments of the history of the Church — defeat of Attila the Hun, coronation of Charlemagne, schism with the Greek Orthodox Church, time of Luther — that Cécile was a Christian Martyr in Imperial Rome and that Henriette was a French princess who was instrumental in the re-establishment of Roman Catholicism in England in the seventeenth century, just after the death of Leo X (the Pope Delmont resembles most) adds depth and resonance to the original marital problem which seemed at first to be the subject of *La Modification*. Names are used as signposts to the characters and as stimuli to the imagination of the reader — Grumeaux, Delétang, de Vere, Revel, Buck.[7]

At first Butor uses individuals to symbolize groups, but later in his work he strips them of name and identity and uses the real groups themselves as naked forces: whites, negros and Indians in *Mobile*, the American people again in *6 810 000 litres d'eau par seconde*. The characters of *6 810 000 litres* have names, certainly, but are shown their role by the initial which indicates their type. At other times Butor encircles an individual with more or less distorted images of himself. (We remember the cover of *L'Arc*.) These may be other characters, heroes in myth or in literature, who help the character to understand himself better, and the reader to recognize the much wider repercussion of his presence in such a situation.

Here we recognize, as well as an expression of the way man is seen from many angles, Butor's own search for self-consciousness. He moves gradually within his work from the use of fictional characters through semi-fictional presentations of himself in *Portrait de l'artiste en jeune singe* and *Votre Faust*, to a use of his own person in *Où*, *Travaux d'approche* and *Matière de Rêves*. He gains the ability to present himself in his writing and thus affirms his being in the world.

If we study this evolution in detail, we shall learn not only a great deal about the author himself, but also, and more important, Butor's technique for coming to grips with himself as an individual who is also an object in other people's worlds. Once we have understood this problem, which is shared by us all, and learned to see the multiple roles imposed by society as aspects of an ever variable unity

8

which is not fragmented but full of interesting possibilities, then we may extend this concept to the perceived world and become much more flexible in our attitude towards it. Butor's presentation of himself runs parallel to his presentation of the world. Let us look first at the microcosm of his own self.

The original split between a person's conception of himself and that held by the world around him is to be found in its simplest form in the character of Abel, the black servant in *La Conversation.*[8]

In this story the narrator finds himself in a garden where he is treated by the two other characters in a fashion which disconcerts him. Gradually he realizes that he is in another age and that he is a black servant by the name of Abel. He understands the language the lady and gentleman use between themselves but not the one the lady uses to address him directly, nor does he associate himself with the servant within whose skin he finds himself and whose duties he performs. Time seems to change very rapidly, the couple in period costume fade away, the narrator is mysteriously evicted from the park and the gates turn into a wall behind him. It all seems like a dream.

Here we see the major elements which preoccupy Butor in his four novels presented in a more concentrated form than elsewhere. Abel is black and a servant, ignored for the most part or accepted as a decorative and amusing plaything, but he is the means by which the couple see the disintegration of their world; he fetches and holds the spyglass through which they observe its fall. His role then comes to an end. Developed beyond Ahmed whose part in *Passage de Milan* is equally decorative and equally destructive, he is linked by his name to Cain in *L'Emploi du Temps* and thence to the author and to Horace Buck. He has been fragmented further still.

Buck is much wilder than either of his predecessors; not for him the fancy costume of a houseboy. Though he is treated as an inferior by the white population of Bleston, he is free and thus is feared rather than dominated. He fascinates Jacques Revel and teaches him to react in the way Burton dares to do only under a pseudonym. Whereas Abel shows no reaction to his lot and Ahmed is afraid of losing his position, Buck is in a constant state of revolt as his name indicates. The difference in attitude notwithstanding he, too, is shown in the pursuit of pleasure. He and Revel drink together, go to the fair and to the amusement parks. He is the prime suspect when fires destroy the places of amusement in Bleston; Revel is implicated too because he destroys the negative of George Burton

9

and burns the map of Bleston. Both Buck and Revel are hence joined by fire to the Bleston depicted in the stained glass window in the cathedral and hence to Cain, his destruction of the old order, life as an outcast and construction of a new order of townlife in which the arts have a place. Abel and Burton must go to make way for Cain and Revel.

The fourth coloured character created by Butor, the North African in *Degrés*, is less obviously connected to either pleasure or destruction but has considerable potential for either. His face covered with sticking plaster, silent and threatening, he haunts Pierre Eller and Alain Mouron. They connect him to Vernier and thus he becomes an author figure again, upsetting their daily life. He generates a fear similar to that connected to Buck so that he also cannot be separate from Eller's revolt against his uncle.

These characters are all cut off from the others by their race. Colour serves to exaggerate alienation from society, as does difference of tongue. In *La Conversation* these characteristics are combined in one character but in the novels this is not so, and if there is a problem of disorientation through language it is the protagonist who suffers from it. This is the case of Jacques Revel and also of Léon Delmont.

Now the development from the story to the novels becomes clear. The narrator is at odds with the people around him and with his own body. At first he does not realize that the lady and gentleman are discussing him, then he feels that he is usurping the role of someone else. This division is augmented in the other works mentioned above: the coloured servant and the narrator form separate characters in the books. The clearest link between them is in *L'Emploi du Temps* where the development of Revel and Buck are parallel throughout. To a large extent Buck is the exteriorization of the growing frustration, resentment and anguish within Revel. He is the dark side of Revel's personality and opens new worlds of experience to the Frenchman (amusement arcade). Revel meets Buck by accident and for a long time does not even know his name yet they are linked by their fight against the power of Bleston. Burton and Jenkins cannot accept him.

In the same way the North African personifies all that the schoolboys sense and fear in Pierre Vernier, the emotion and power they feel to be a threat to them. Vernier and the North African share the characteristics of the wolf, the leanness, hunger and potential for destruction that Caesar fears in Cassius (*Degrés*, p. 379) and that is applied to both of them by the texts the students in Eller's class are reading.[9] The North African appears rarely in *Degrés* but he is a haunting, menacing figure who bears the same relation to the author-protagonist as does Buck.

Léon Delmont has an alter-ego of a slightly different kind. He is the "Grand Veneur", spirit of the forest of Fontainbleau. This supernatural figure is not given a colour in *La Modification* but is described in legend as being always dressed in black and/or rags, seated on a black horse with flaming nostrils. His passage brings death in its wake. The questions posed by the "Grand Veneur" give direction to the self-interrogation of Delmont, and in the dream the characters fuse together,[10] forming one divided identity which once more approaches the internal split in Abel's outlook.

The main character of each novel has more than one reflection of himself within his immediate world, with the exception of Ahmed who seems rather to reflect characteristics of the people around him. Revel finds his tutelary in Cain and is thus associated with a host of possible developments — destruction of a world, guilt, exile, Cain as father of the black races — leading back once more to Abel in *La Conversation* and out into a multitude of biblical and literary variations on the theme. Likewise, we measure Delmont against Julian the Apostate, whose letters he reads and the pattern of whose life greatly resembles his own. The parallel is becoming more literary, more precise. The trend is continued in *Degrés* where Vernier is surrounded by texts in which aspects of his situation and character are visible. It is possible to substitute his relationship with Eller into any of the plays read by the class or by IA, and hence their problems are shown from a multitude of angles. The class substitutes Vernier into *Julius Caesar* and sees him both as Caesar the tyrant and also as Cassius, while Vernier himself sees Eller as Brutus who betrays him whichever role he plays. IIA also sees Vernier as Nero and Eller as Britannicus his victim, while contemplation of *L'Ecole des Femmes* offers another aspect entirely.

The novels have turned full circle around *La Conversation*. All its elements have been developed in various directions; the original character, divided within itself, has been split apart totally as a result of its desperate struggle to deal with the advance of time and pressure of the physical environment. Dream has given way to reality. At this point Butor's work divides into those books which study the environment in detail (*Le Génie du Lieu, Description de San Marco, Mobile*) and those concerned with the individual leading directly to the ultimate presentation of the elements observed in the novels: *Votre Faust*.

The Faust legend contains all the themes discussed: the splitting of one personality into the characters of Faust and Mephistopheles (who is black by implication), the desire for understanding through language and books, and the desperate struggle against time. Throughout the novels Butor, through his characters, strives to capture understanding of a moment, of a life; surely such absolute knowledge is what Faust tries to obtain. It seems inevitable that Butor should write his *Faust*, as both he and his protagonist share also a devastating awareness of the mobility of life and the infiniteness of questioning. Butor writes in his poem "Pérégrination":

> Je savais bien que la question
> N'était pas ma possession
> Mais mon élément
> Elle est ma terre
> Et le fruit même de l'arbre
> Où l'on m'a déposé dès ma naissance
> Je n'en suis nullement l'origine
> Mais la victime
> Et le résultat[11]

Butor's *Faust*[12] uses all the elements we have seen already and develops them to the full. Not content with one Faust and one Mephistopheles, he multiplies them to infinity. Henri, the musician who has always written church music, is approached by the Director who commissions an opera from him. The Director will pay him handsomely during the period of composition, however long that may be, but there is one condition — the opera must be a *Faust* and he, the Director, will provide the libretto. Here we have our modern Faust and his Mephisto who will re-enact the episode between Faust and Gretchen, for Henri has a girl-friend, Maggy, who sings at the "Cabaret de l'Eglise" and whom he abandons for an opera singer. He then travels a great deal: we have reference to Goethe's *Faust* and Thomas Mann's *Dr. Faustus*. Because Henri is writing an opera he hears a number of rehearsals where snatches from many musical visits to the underworld may be heard yet strangely none of the musical quotations are from *Faust* operas. On his wanderings he visits a fairground and sees the old Faust puppet play. Just as Butor's other characters have found reflections of themselves in history, myth and literature, so Henri is surrounded by all previous manifestations of himself and his dilemma.

The various levels of experience are offered not only in quotation but in presentation. Behind the sequence of scenes between Henri, Maggy and the Director can be heard the literary quotations and also a continuum of Henri's own voice disputing with himself the propriety of his actions. Hence he is divided simultaneously both historically and internally within the present.

The problem of comprehension is codified in the treatment of language. As in *Description de San Marco* modern foreign languages are used to indicate that which is part of human experience though at present unknown (we remember the plight of Abel, Revel and Delmont), while Latin expresses the superhuman — hence the hymns to God and the Devil. These are intertwined in *Votre Faust*.

Henri-Faust is bombarded with all possible information about his own past which he should be able to use in his attempts to understand the present. And this time the protagonist is not alone to face his problems, as Delmont was when surrounded by his past — the projection of experience expands beyond the stage alone.

Henri Pousseur, who wrote the music for the opera, also wrote Henri's opening speech and hence is linked to the character in thought as well as by name. This clearly leaves the role of the Director for Butor himself, as each provides the libretto for his musician. Author and composer are implicated in the attitudes and actions of their fictional counterparts. In addition the work is called *Votre Faust*. Just as Henri is immersed in the experience of the total Faust, so is the audience, for on four occasions they are called upon to decide how the plot should proceed: twice by vote and twice by the decision of individuals from amongst them. They too must choose whether or not to abandon Maggy, and they are given three opportunities to reverse their original decision. In this way the characters are divided between many versions, as is the actor for he can hear himself speaking two sets of lines. The composer, the author and the audience watch themselves on stage as they sit in the auditorium. Each individual Faustian experience has been fragmented and all the pieces reassembled into a whole which incorporates everybody. Butor does not allow us to watch Faust; we must participate in his dilemma as does Butor himself, and as he has in one way or another in all his previous fiction.

Votre Faust is the culmination of Butor's attitude to literature until that time. It is his final statement of the problem of the acquisition of knowledge, the growth of understanding and the unification of the individual to date. Five years after the publication of *Votre*

Faust appeared Butor's first attempt to reach a solution, *Portrait de l'artiste en jeune singe*, a capriccio and semi-autobiographical piece. The juxtaposition which has been seen until now between fictional characters is again the basis of this book. *Portrait* is divided between reality and dream. (Alternate chapters are devoted to each; roman and italic type make the distinction obvious at all times.) The main character, the one who experiences the reality and dreams the dreams, is Butor himself as a young man. For the first time the author is writing in his own name and no other person in the book is used to fill out any aspect of his character. The division that we have seen throughout his work has not disappeared, rather there has been a return to the situation in *La Conversation*. Once again the rupture is within one person. Butor's double lives in his dreams and is a literary character of the kind found in *La Modification* and in *Degrés*. The split no longer plays an active role in the character's daily life but is only present in his unconscious mind.

The young Butor's double is the hero of the Second Calender's Tale in *The Thousand and One Nights*. This prince in exile meets a woodcutter and learns his trade. Out working one day he finds a princess imprisoned underground. The genie who is holding her captive turns the prince into a monkey and in this guise the prince wins a writing competition, for he knows a number of scripts, and thus becomes secretary to a king whose daughter breaks the spell by winning in her turn a contest with the genie; the monkey then regains his human form but the princess dies.

Butor himself is away in Germany at this time, and the count-librarian with whom he is staying dresses frequently as a forester. The young man learns a number of languages and with this knowledge studies alchemy. The monkey is a recognizable symbol of the alchemist who considers himself the ape of God. Hence the end of the period of bewitchment marks the end of the initiation period in Butor's studies. He is then free to move on.

In *Portrait de l'artiste en jeune singe* the literary parallel is not presented openly though clues are given; Butor finds a copy of *The Thousand and One Nights* in every library he uses, and attention is drawn to it — in one instance by the ringing of an alarm bell. Snatches of the story occur in the dreams, mingled with details from the young man's activities and readings during the day. It is for the reader to recognize the analogy and use it as he wishes.

The division seems to be between the conscious and unconcious mind, between reality and dream, but now the two elements resemble each other much more closely than they did in the earlier books. The Calender's story adds resonance to the surface development of the book but does not move in any direction of its own. Gone is the opposing pull between Buck and Revel, gone the fascination Mephistopheles exerts over Faust. The young Butor's worlds run parallel and their interaction is complementary. Within them he is still very conscious of the passage of time and the work conveys an impression of haste. Each chapter takes place on a different day of the week and each is a week and a day after the previous one. Also the character is again a stranger in a foreign land, but this time he speaks the language and is able to communicate with the people around him. The problems which were important in the earlier works are still present in *Portrait*, but they are no longer sources of anguish.

In *Où* Butor again speaks in his own name, this time in the present. Still he is in foreign lands but the cultural division offers more enrichment than conflict. Early in the book, caught in a rainstorm in the ruins of Angkor, Butor comes face to face with a native flute player who is strongly reminiscent of Ahmed and Abel. Butor does not speak to the flute player and thus the remains of the link between the author (hero) and his (black) alter-ego are broken. The time of personal fragmentation seems to be over. No longer are the characters divided either physically or emotionally. No longer is a break made between the author and his characters. Butor seems to have found an integrated identity and the freedom to express it. A fusion has been achieved.[13]

The characters have served one of their purposes by being the means by which Butor expressed and resolved his problem as an individual in the world. They have served another by making the reader very conscious of the links between people, their surroundings and their civilization. A further purpose is that by seeing characters reflected in others and also in literary and mythical personnages we realize how closely our world and that of literature and history are connected. There is no division between an author's real experience and his "imaginary" works; fiction is an extension of reality and so is dream. Both develop possibilities inherent in relationships, situations and events and are powerful tools in man's understanding.

As we see, Butor's is a work that is tightly interwoven; each element within it has two aspects, real and imaginary. Just as the planes go round the world in opposite directions in *Réseau Aérien*, just as Fourier's world has a masculine, major development before "death" and a feminine, minor one afterwards in *La Rose des Vents*, so life as a whole has its counterpart in literature, the individual consciousness is backed by dream. Every book of Butor's which has individually drawn characters contains at least one dream, and these dreams hold keys to the protagonist's state of mind. This is made clear already in *Passage de Milan* where the dreaming hours are juxtaposed to the waking ones and another side of the dreamer is shown. Louis Lécuyer dreams his shattered illusions concerning Angèle as she turns from the pure bride to a sensual being whose face disintegrates before Louis' eyes while the Virgin Mary turns into Bast, the Egyptian goddess of love. Louis himself sinks into the ground, swallowed up by the very sand of Egypt — the essence of sensuality and wisdom in the symbolic pattern of the novel. Jean Ralon travels through the Egyptian Otherworld in his dream, with Ahmed as his guide and mentor. He has lost his faith in Christianity (Revel and Buck). Alexis displays a lack of belief too: the boat he is in drifts away from land and sinks while Louis calls Alexis from the shore.

The dreams in *L'Emploi du Temps* are similar to those above, but Delmont's dream in *La Modification* is more sustained, presenting his situation in a series of images which help him come to a solution of his problem. It is not until *Portrait*, however, that the power of the subconscious and of the imagination is given its full importance. The young Butor's daily activities are elaborated and interpreted nightly by dreams which are given equal space, alternating chapter by chapter with reality. Here the two forces work together in the formation of the young man. Perhaps the author completed a description of Charles Fourier's universe, not only to lend his voice to the plea that imagination should not be denied, but also to show at the same time the danger inherent in excessive imagination should it be given free rein in society.

References to Fourier and to dream bring us to André Breton to whom *La Rose des Vents* is dedicated, and who wrote an *Ode à Charles Fourier*. Surrealism has had a certain influence on Butor which can be seen in his poetry in particular (e.g. *Petites Liturgies Intimes pour hâter l'avènement du Grand Transparent de Jacques Hérold*). In his youth he frequented the galleries of the Left Bank and knew many of the group around Breton. He wrote critical studies on a number of the artists (Zañartu, Hérold). This influence was counter-balanced by studies in philosophy, (notably in phenomenology), the selection of a thesis topic "Mathematics and the Idea of Necessity" under the supervision of Gaston Bachelard, then the translation of A. Gurwitz's book *Theory of the Field of Consciousness*. In Butor's life, as in his work as typified by *L'Arc* No. 39, a careful balance has been preserved between the real and the imaginary, between *Le Livre des figures d'Abraham* and the *Book of Kells* (*L'Arc*, pp. 86, 99), La Pointe du Raz and Mars (*L'Arc*, pp. 24-31, 36-40). We shall see, as this study continues, the importance of the role of the one as catalyst to the other in the maintenance of an active appreciation of our position in our world, of Butor in his.

Throughout this chapter, we have considered the self-reflexive quality of Michel Butor's work. The fragmentation and reduplication of characters, the re-appearance of themes in ever shifting guises, the use of symbolic echos which have resonance at multifarious levels of understanding, evoke relationships within and between the many books the author has produced to date and above all link, the twin forces of reality and imagination. Butor's experience is an essential part of his writing given that his main aim is the systematic exploration of his surroundings in all their geographical extent, historical density and cultural variety, in order to achieve a greater appreciation of the richness offered and express what he has gained in such a way that he shares his knowledge, while at the same time maintaining both the clarity of his vision and the complexity of his material. Butor offers us an initiation similar to his own if we are prepared to make a similar effort — an initiation into the interpretive and revelatory power of literature as the world finds a reflection of itself in linguistic symbols.

CHAPTER I: FOOTNOTES

[1] Cf. G. Raillard, *Michel Butor* (Paris: Gallimard, collection "Idées", 1968), for an excellent biographical and bibliographical study.

[2] *L'Arc*, No. 39 (November 1969). *L'Arc* is a periodical published three times a year in Aix-en-Provence. Each of its numbers is devoted to a special artist or topic influential in the twentieth century. See Appendix I for a breakdown of the contents of the Butor issue.

[3] *L'Arc*, p. 2: "There are no personal works. The work of an individual is a sort of knot produced inside a cultural web into which the individual is not plunged but rather within which he appeared. Right from the start the individual is a moment in this cultural web. Moreover any work is always a collective work." (All translations are my own.)

[4] For editions of Michel Butor's works referred to in this book see Bibliography.

5 G. Charbonnier, *Entretiens avec Michel Butor* (Paris: Gallimard, 1967), pp. 27-28: "One must listen out for reality, seize the moment when reality begins to speak ... one must seize the moments when something we did not understand begins to reveal itself to us, when something becomes clear to us."

6 For further examples see J. Walters, "Symbolism in *Passage de Milan*," *French Review*, XLII, 2 (December 1968), pp. 223-32.

7 For development of this point see J. Walters, "La Recherche géographique et historique de l'identité butorienne," *Marche Romane* (Liège), XXI, 1-2 (1971), pp. 58-61.

8 *Les Cahiers des Saisons*, No. 9 (1957) (short story).

9 See below, Chapter VI: Livres.

10 *La Modification*, pp. 179, 191, 210.

11 *Tel Quel* (Autumn 1961), p. 74: "I well knew that the question/ was not my possession/ but my element/ it is my earth/ the very fruit of the tree/ where I was placed at birth/ I am in no way its origin/ but its victim/ and result."

12 For a more complete description see below Chapter V: Spectacles.

13 Since this was written Butor has treated the theme once more and in dream form again. In a short story called "Le rêve de l'huître," *Matière de Rêves* (Paris: Gallimard, 1975), Butor metamorphoses from himself Michel Butor author on a lecture tour into the body and role of a black servant Bernard before regaining his own identity once more. See *Malahat Review* No. 32 (1974) for a translated version.

CHAPTER II

Arts et métiers

The first thing we notice when we look at a copy of *L'Arc* No. 39 is the striking cover, the collage by Jiri Kolár mentioned above, which presents a multi-faceted Michel Butor surrounded by words. Immediately upon opening the volume the similarity of form between the prehistoric tool on the obverse of the cover (a jade disk with a hole in the middle — Plate 3) and the work of art on the front impresses itself upon our awareness. If we then turn to the paragraph concerning the tool (p. 12) we find that jade is a symbol of life and that the hole in the centre symbolizes the sky and also the power of the emperor. This explanation is opposite a modern machine which has perhaps the same limits and powers: the plan of a computer. These three juxtaposed illustrations set the poles with which Butor is concerned and the way he chooses to present his idea. He must span the extent from the oldest inventions made by man to the most modern, the artisanal skill and the imagination that directs it, for on them our world is based. To these he must join the many aspects of man (and of himself not least) all captured within the mobile network which is language. If he succeeds he has power over all things, the sky is within his grasp.

The rest of the section of "Arts et Métiers" in *L'Arc* explores the above subjects from different angles, in disconnected sections; its impact is built from skilful presentation of contrasting elements. Beginning with a person whose interests are seen to radiate out to join with those of other people thus joining a number of groups which in turn lead to others, the different divisions of *L'Arc* illustrate what the skill of man has produced: tombs and restaurants, music and science, exercise of intellect and imagination, leading to an understanding of the world itself. (The suggestions for exploration go from *L'Astronome* to *le butor étoilé*.) From this base anything can be accomplished. Butor suggests changes in the sky: musical satellites, coloured rain, symphonies of wind over the desert — all of which remind us of Charles Fourier's universe and Butor's own contribution, *La Rose des Vents*. *L'Arc* leads from mundane tasks (the salesgirl in the Galeries Lafayette) to cosmic possibilities, and Butor suggests that anyone who learns his trade well and practises it with flair (which in his own case is that he should understand his society, draw out its most important elements and present them clearly in his books) can in time accomplish his wildest dreams. But like the citizens in Fourier's world he cannot accomplish them alone. *L'Arc* No. 39 is a work of collaboration under Butor's direction: present-day authors provide sections of their own devising, certain writers from the past are selected and quoted, and the works or figments of imagination of others are referred to. All are brought together with consummate skill in order that the selected ideas may enlighten the reader, stimulate his fancy and open new facets of his world.

Butor's is an art of juxtaposition. Always his works are full of quotations, references to works of art, books, places to visit, all of which have bearing upon his own work. No detail in Butor's writing should be ignored; knowledge of anything he mentions, be it simply in passing, will enrich the reader's understanding of the situation within the work. Every book quoted in *Degrés* throws light on the relationship between Vernier and Eller, or develops the theme of discovery. Every quotation in *Votre Faust*, be it literary or musical, helps Henri-Faust-audience to a solution of the dilemma. Every author or mineral listed in *Portrait de l'artiste en jeune singe* advances the young Butor on his quest. And Butor's is not an esoteric attitude. Read chronologically, he teaches the reader how to deal with his books; the example is given quite clearly in Revel's use of *Bleston Murder* and developed again in the second and third parts of *Degrés* where the quotations given are applied directly to the situation in the classroom by the boys themselves.

Butor's métier is that of a writer of poetry, fiction and criticism, so these are the skills which he studies both in theory and practice.[1] For him the writer has a social responsibility, as much of our grasp of reality comes from what we read. On the one hand much of what we read is false, so that we must make ourselves aware of the distinction between imaginary and real situations — a distinction which it is very difficult to make as our reality is constantly being modified by increasing knowledge; on the other hand description of fictional situations fills out our experience and helps us to deal with circumstances otherwise beyond our grasp.

The novel (as the prime fictional structure) is in a delicate position between reality and dream. It has a function which is tightly linked to the former and yet its very essence is that of imagination, fantasy and dream. As a result it tends to have a double level of implication, a division which Butor explores in certain of his early essays. In "L'alchimie et son language" (*Répertoire*) he discusses hidden levels of meaning within language, the use of cypher, analogy and known symbol to transmit information below the surface of the story told. "La balance des fées" carries this into the interpretation of actions, suggesting that fairytales teach two distinct moralities to children. Authors have thus the power to turn reality into illusion or to offer within dreams a key to the understanding of actual situations. The writer's function is to reveal reality (which conversely gives him the ability to mystify) by means of his imaginative force. One writer can create a whole world (Balzac, Proust), but if writers shared the decors they create then their power within society would be greatly increased. This is suggested in "La crise de croissance de la Science-Fiction." (We begin to see why Butor draws on other authors all the time.)

The novel both constitutes in itself a mythology within society upon which everyone can draw and also clarifies and elucidates those myths which are created by society, expressive of its problems and contradictions and yet unrecognized, diffuse, until the novelist formulates them for his reader. In this way the novelist is inevitably a critic of his society and he can choose either of the two forms the novel can take, either of the roles it can play; he can formulate tranquillizers for the problems he sees around him, encouraging his reader to accept illusory solutions, or he can force the reader to become aware of the source of the situation and help him to deal with it in a positive fashion. In this way the novel becomes a means of exploration, engaging the author and reader in the reality which surrounds them, filling gaps in the information held by the latter and offering methods of expressing it to others.

Each new reality needs to be expressed in its own particular way so that the writer who has accepted his interpretative role with relation to his society must search continually for new forms of fiction which are capable of encompassing the new problems, new myths within the context created by previous realities and previous fictions, for no author, in a world as full of books as ours, can possibly imagine that he stands alone. The problems posed by reality thus appear to the writer transposed into a series of technical difficulties. If he can resolve these difficulties, the form being an integral part of the contents of the work, he will have found and expressed the way to deal with the original problems within society. Any literary structure and style born of an attitude to a reality provides a method for dealing with that reality; for that reason any writer who recognizes and accepts the exploratory and didactic nature of his art must struggle to refine his tools as much as possible.

Michel Butor does this both in practice inside his fictions and in theory in his criticism. The author's problems are shown within the novels, particularly those in which a narrator-hero is attempting to write a description of reality as he sees it. Revel struggles to situate himself within time and space, Delmont finds reflections of himself in art and history, while Vernier searches desperately for a way to describe the innumerable inter-relations of a group of people. None of them manages to express his world in its complexity in any other way than by juxtaposition of its elements.

C'est en *essayant* entre eux des fragments d'événements que le sens naît, c'est en transformant inlassablement ces événements en fonctions que la structure s'édifie: comme le bricoleur, l'écrivain (poète, romancier ou chroniqueur) ne *voit* le sens des unités inertes qu'il a devant lui qu'en les rapportant . . .[2]

Roland Barthes wrote these words about *Mobile*, Butor's representation of the USA, but the principle involved is one which is fundamental to all his work. Everything Butor writes is concerned with the complexity of the world and the difficulty which faces man when he tries to understand what is happening around him. The amount of information to be considered before any kind of conclusion can be reached is immense. Simplification usually brings distortion, and as Butor states in *Passage de Milan*:

C'est seulement lorsque les choses se compliquent qu'elles commencent à apparaître clairement.[3] (*Ed. M.*)

Butor's major preoccupation as a novelist is to find a way to transmit a sense of complexity while helping his readers to cope with that which surrounds them every day.

The essays in *Répertoire* are concerned with problems of expression. Butor begins with an essay defining the role of the novel in which he writes:

J'appelle "symbolisme" d'un roman, l'ensemble des relations de ce qu'il nous décrit avec la réalité où nous vivons.
Ces relations ne sont pas les mêmes selon les romans, et il me semble

que la tâche essentielle du critique est de les débrouiller, de les éclaircir afin que l'on puisse extraire de chaque oeuvre particulière tout son enseignement . . . Le symbolisme externe du roman tend à se réfléchir dans un symbolisme interne, certaines parties jouant, par rapport à l'ensemble, le même rôle que celui-ci par rapport à la réalité.[4] (*Ed. M.*)

The next nineteen essays examine ways in which various authors or genres have created their own "symbolism", reflecting their world in the way described above. By examining certain of the relations between the structural and stylistic elements within each work, Butor proceeds to extract all that the author's circumstances and attitude have to offer him. His reading of them is meticulous: no detail is so small that it may be left out of account when the author's intentions are being considered, his universe reconstructed. (And from Butor's reading of others, his readers must learn how to read his writings in their turn.) Also, the authors discussed in *Répertoire* are presented in chronological order so that their experiments and literary daring may be seen as strata building up towards the practices of the present day as surely as the history of their time lays foundations for epochs that follow. The organization of the essays creates a relationship between them which in itself adds to the importance of each and strengthens the impact of the whole. As defined above, the relations within each study reflect those between the essays and that of the book in the work of Butor and his time.

Indeed the last essay, "Intervention à Royaumont", describes Butor's personal attitude to the form he has been examining within the book. He explains that the writing of a novel is for him a way to give unity to his life when events and objects threaten to overwhelm him. The novel then becomes the exteriorization of struggles and problems, and its resolution the achievement of a temporary liberation for the author. Inevitably then, the author's own development will be traceable through his work together with that of the society which provoked the original dilemma. Hence the novel is the product of one reality and the expression of a second; but as it was not written for the author alone, but for the people around him who were also involved in the circumstances which instigated the writing, then it should produce among them a reaction which will modify their attitudes, create further realities and ask a new question which will in its turn produce books in response — criticism turning back upon the first work, new novels moving on to find solutions to the problems the first poses.

So Butor's work moves in two directions simultaneously and

23

responds to two needs: the author's need to discover his own position in a complex world and his wish to help his readers do likewise. *Répertoire* reviews literature of the past at a time when Butor's first four novels are exploring the problems posed by the modern world with its vast network of communications which permits constant access to wider ranges of time and space than ever before.

Many of Butor's reflections on his work can be found in *Répertoire II*, a volume which is again arranged with great care. Turning on the pivot of the central essay, "Le Critique et son public," the first part of the book is concerned with theoretical considerations which are put into practice in the second part. The last chapter comprises an interview, bringing the reader back to Butor's own work, to the direct application of what he has read and to the personal note on which the book opens. The theoretical writings offer a complete introduction to the important elements of the author's own work: the role of the novel, its presentation of time, space and people, and the book itself as an object. First the role of the novel and its possible poetic force are examined. Like poetry, the novel should be able to make important elements of life distinct from the others, to renew and perpetuate the values which are necessary to the life of the society from which it is drawn and whose structure it makes clear.

Le romancier alors est celui qui aperçoit qu'une structure est en train de s'esquisser dans ce qui l'entoure, et qui va poursuivre cette structure, la faire croître, la perfectionner, l'étudier, jusqu'au moment où elle sera lisible pour tous.[5] (*Ed. M.*)

Hence no element of a novel should be discounted as fortuitous or superfluous. Everything in the book should be in relation to an aspect of the reality outside it.

Butor is interested primarily in relationships: those of the book itself as a myth-making force in society, and that of literature among the arts. For him music and art have great interpretative powers too (we see them at work within his fiction); reflecting and refracting reality, they form part of the network of communication supported mainly by language. Both are inseparable from words (*Les Mots dans la Peinture*, "Les mots dans la musique," *Musique en Jeu* No. 4) and so in fact have no domain apart from the one they share with language as means of expression of man's experience. Butor maintains that music is as realistic a form as the others and draws on musical structure quite considerably as a basis for his work.

24

The novels are influenced by the form of the canon where one voice recalls the part sung by another. (This is the key to Butor's use of memory.[6]) *Description de San Marco* bears the mark of Stravinsky's *Canticum Sacrum in honorem Sancti Marci nominis*, a work, like Butor's own, born of and in explanation of St. Mark's Basilica.

Music, of course, helps to deal with the problem of time and hence of space. The events in the apartments in *Passage de Milan* are juxtaposed like so many instruments in an orchestra, so many parts in a score. So are the events remembered by Revel and Delmont, and the books to which Vernier refers. Butor writes in "L'espace du roman":

Depuis quelques années la critique commence à reconnaître la valeur privilégiée du travail romanesque dans l'exploration de la dimension temporelle, l'étroite parenté de cet art avec un autre se déployant avant tout dans le temps: la musique. A partir d'un certain niveau de réflexion, on est obligé de s'apercevoir que la plupart des problèmes musicaux ont des correspondants dans l'ordre romanesques, que les structures musicales ont des applications romanesques . . . Musique et roman s'éclairent mutuellement.[7] (*Ed. M.*)

Hence a relationship between music and the novel is offered for exploration. Both struggle with the effects of time on reality and ways in which the multiple inter-relations can be expressed. Likewise the novel is concerned with the presentation of space and thus has similar links with painting and the other arts which explore it. In this way the novel becomes the intermediate term between reality and non-verbal representations of it as well as a pivot between the non-linguistic arts themselves. Such a position implies a tremendous flexibility and incorporative force such as that attributed by Butor to the novel within the realm of language. He writes:

Si nous sommes capables de les relier les unes aux autres [les phrases de tous les jours] à l'intérieur de formes fortes, ces phrases, si banales à première vue, vont se révéler comme ayant une signification que nous avons oubliée, ou que nous n'avions pas su entendre.[8] (*Ed. M.*)

The novel thus becomes the communicative form par excellence.

Butor experiments systematically with the presentation of time. The events of *Passage de Milan* take twelve hours to unfold and the book is divided into twelve chapters, a clock being heard to strike in each. The length of the chapters differs according to the subjective attitude to time of the characters within each one. The story is told more or less chronologically though it is fragmented by movement in space. The past is represented by the objects surrounding

25

Léonard and the Ralons and when it is necessary to understand the accident, Léonard asks Lécuyer to retell what happened in full. All the elements which are explored in the later works are present: clock time versus subjective time, history, memory and the close relation between time and space. Understanding is born of a total understanding of the past. All these elements become more complicated in *L'Emploi du Temps*[9] — a journal of his year in Bleston begun by Jacques Revel after seven months of his stay are over. He decides that it is essential for the survival of his personality that he should recapture the time that has passed. He begins in May to describe happenings of the previous October, hoping to recreate them fully and so come to an understanding of their significance. This idea of repetition is one Butor discussed in his essays on Kierkegaard, and the pattern of writing which Revel hopes to establish (that of capturing each month events which occurred seven months previously) is very similar to that of Frater Taciturnius in *Stages on Life's Way*.[10] The monk writes every morning what happened twelve months earlier and in the evening records the events of the day; thus he gives the present its due throughout and Revel is soon obliged to do likewise.

L'Emploi du Temps is divided into five sections corresponding to the remaining months of Revel's stay in Bleston. Each section is divided into five chapters corresponding to the weeks of the month, the first section beginning on the first day of the month and continuing until the end of the week, however short a time this may be. The following three sections take a full week beginning on Monday and the last covers the remaining days. Each section is subdivided into days and dated. Revel usually writes every weekday but on one occasion writes on Saturday. Sometimes, when under great emotional strain, he misses days.

He intends to follow the pattern set up in May, so that during the course of each month he will cover events of seven months before and if possible advance rapidly enough to catch up with the present. He succeeds in his plan for the first month, but during the second he cannot avoid writing about present happenings as well as those of November. The whole project thus becomes more and more complicated as Revel finds that he is unable to look at the past as he understood it at the time; more recent events throw light upon the more distant ones. It is imperative that these connections be shown at the time of describing the first event of any particular series; events of seven months before are incomprehensible without knowl-

26

edge of others which arose in the intermediate time between them and the present. To express this clearly would be problem enough if Revel were working from a fixed point, but the advancing present continues to provide information about the past so that partially recaptured periods need to be rewritten constantly as more complete knowledge forces a reinterpretation of the facts. The result is that in the first section Revel is concerned with a single level of narration, in the second two, the third three. . . . Gradually various major events emerge clearly from the surrounding chaos and become isolated centres of memory, key patches in the year arising from the confusion of the forgotten periods.

Revel is working under a number of different time pressures which pull towards the end of his stay, to the beginning and to key events within the year. He is striving to keep abreast of the present and not to fall behind in his schedule of writing in order to achieve his aim of finishing the work before the end of the year. He cannot possibly accomplish this, and is writing furiously about February, still an unexplored month, when seated in the train waiting to leave the town. Thus the book ends with a question: what could have happened in February?

A consciousness of the pressure of time and the complicated interweaving of different periods are thus two of the major preoccupations of the book. As the author-hero moves from month to month the impression is that of being overwhelmed, being lost in an ever-increasing labyrinth of inter-connecting facts and periods which the author-hero is trying vainly to chart. The past of Bleston, the simultaneous presentation of several consecutive events in the tapestries, the distant past in the stained glass windows and the films all add to Revel's confusion and the reader's realization of the complexity of the element described. Burton's explanation of the technique of the detective story is a guide to all concerned.[11]

La Modification offers a control experiment of the same problem. Delmont is surrounded by his past and his future in his memory, in the people in his train compartment, the art and architecture of Paris and Rome. But the advancing present which caused Revel's downfall is controlled for Delmont by the train timetable. He is in a bubble of chronology and thus able to reflect on the events around him.

Degrés is bedevilled by the present again as Vernier tries to capture a school year with its intricate hourly structure.[12] *6 810 000 litres d'eau par seconde* is also a description of a year, this time governed

27

by the changing seasons at Niagara Falls. Such recurrent cycles (we think of the fair moving around Bleston) are often to be found in Butor's work in conjunction with historic periods and clock time, showing the forces which both control and modify the reality which the characters perceive subjectively. The passengers in *Réseau Aérien* are victims of an upset of one of these apparently stable scales — clocktime — as they fly around the world. So is the reader of *Mobile* because by taking the states in alphabetical order and spending one hour in each, the usual advance of the day is perturbed.

Most of the books are built on a counterpoint of historical periods, evoked by literature, art and architecture, and all push the reader on into the future. Interest in time works in both directions for Butor, because the future inevitably contains the past and the past is pregnant with the future. (See the discussion between Léonard and his friends in *Passage de Milan*.) Hence it is to Fourier that he turns for the basis of his evocation of the development of the universe. *La Rose des Vents* is constructed in four sections, on the musical scale with a system of pivots and sub-pivots articulating the various parts. Similarly its world goes through eight periods from Eden to Harmony four times in ascending and descending movements to the end of an epoch.

Time gives meaning to distance, geographical as well as historical; distance gives a sense of continuity to time. Space can be represented more conveniently because it lends itself to analogy with geometry but in fact no space can ever be pure geometric form because all human space is necessarily historic; hence when a person moves from place to place his concept of both time and space will be renewed.

Delmont's journey and that of the passengers in *Réseau Aérien* differ because of their mode of transport. Different ways of travelling require different routes, and any space constructed by an author must take such variations into account. Bleston, for example, is a town in which Revel may walk, ride or take a bus; whichever method he chooses he will see his surroundings from a different angle. The difference in perception of space will modify his actions. Likewise the personal space of a house or flat requires different behaviour of its inhabitant in the various rooms. *Passage de Milan* describes small enclosed spaces, *L'Emploi du Temps* moves out into a town, *La Modification* presents the relationship between two cities. *Mobile* shows a network of towns forming a country; *Réseau Aérien*

28

links the whole earth into such a structure. *Le Génie du Lieu,
6 810 000 litres d'eau par seconde* and *Où* initiate the reader into
the mythical power contained within a site, while *Degrés* and
Portrait de l'artiste en jeune singe give this power to a place through
the literature connected to it. Many of Butor's shorter works, essays
like *La première vue de Philadelphie, Palerme, La Gare St Lazare,
Les Montagnes Rocheuses* and *Quatre Lettres écrites du Nouveau
Mexique à Camille Bryen*,[13] explore individual places in detail. For
the author, journeys are fascinating because they teach him more
about the world he lives in and simultaneously encourage him to go
on a mental journey reviewing old ideas, perceiving new facets of
well-known things — *Portrait* is the illustration of this for himself
and the encouragement given to the reader to follow him. Both
points are reinforced in *Les Sept Femmes de Gilbert le Mauvais*
where we see Marcel's rooms leading out into society and into the
depths of the narrator's being.

To use the theme of a journey as the basis for a piece of fiction
is time-honoured for the very reason that a reader will more easily
forsake the reality of his own room to go on a journey, with all the
mental changes this may demand as he accompanies the characters
on their way, than he will make the leap from one stable environment to another. (In the latter case he is more likely to read badly
and not really enter fully into the new world; traces of his own will
deform his perception.) Hence Butor's statement that:

Toute littérature s'inscrit donc en notre espace comme voyage ... tout
roman qui nous raconte un voyage est donc plus clair, plus explicite que
celui qui n'est pas capable d'exprimer métaphoriquement cette distance
entre le lieu de la lecture et celui où nous emmène le récit.[14]   (*Ed. M.*)

The novelist can guide the reader as he will, distorting time and
space so that it will be perceived by the reader in the way the author
wishes. *Mobile* is a case in point because it is not possible to take the
states of the USA in alphabetical order and spend successive hours
in each in turn, yet this presentation serves a definite purpose of
creating awareness both of the vastness of the whole and the similarity within it — any order would do, so the most obvious is chosen.

An author exploits objects in a similar way, using them or their
lack to throw light on characters and events. We remember the
differences between the rooms of Alexis Ralon, Henriette Ledu,
Angèle Vertigues and Gaston Mourre and yet they are all the same
shape, one above the other in the building, and all belong to young

unmarried people. Men live in inhabited space on which the author draws to gain his effects. Butor writes phenomenologically presenting the material world exactly as perceived and leaving it to speak for itself. He said:

Ce qui m'intéresse surtout maintenant, c'est d'essayer de faire parler les choses elles-mêmes, de forcer les choses à la parole. En les disposant d'une certaine façon cela produit des étincelles.[15]

Some objects will then emerge from the confrontation and reveal the significance of the others.

So we are back to Barthes' statement quoted earlier in this chapter; things have an individual importance, but it is in relation to others that their full meaning manifests itself. Patterns and structures must be evolved to clarify the possibility of every detail within those forms; details which will in turn illuminate the form to the full and have repercussions on the reality of the world.

The novelist learns to express the time and space of the world in equivalent literary forms which can connect the reader's time and space, the reading time and space which is the book itself and those of the fiction. He must form similar links between his characters, himself and the reader. Butor discusses the effect of the various personal pronouns within a novel in the essays "L'usage des pronoms personnels" and "Recherches sur la technique du roman" (*Répertoire II*), having put his ideas into practice in the novels. *Passage de Milan* has a third person impersonal observer of the group of characters, *L'Emploi du Temps* a first person narrator who gives a definite point of view to the novel. In *La Modification* and *Degrés* the presentation is more complex. In an interview with Paul Guth, talking about *La Modification*, Butor said:

Il fallait absolument que le récit soit fait au point de vue d'un personnage. Comme il s'agissait d'une prise de conscience, il ne fallait pas que le personnage dise *je*. Il me fallait un monologue intérieur en dessous du niveau du langage du personnage lui-même, dans une forme intermédiare entre la première personne et la troisième. Ce *vous* me permet de décrire la situation du personnage et la façon dont le langage naît en lui.[16]

This would account for the use of the second person, the *vous* in Delmont's monologue which is used to express the subconscious level of action.[17] He produces the thought and also receives it. There is an almost impersonal intercourse between two distinct parts of his mind, in contact yet distant from each other. The ambiguity of the form also creates a link between protagonist and his reader, forcing the latter to involve himself more closely with the hero. Both reader and protagonist are in the position of judge of the other, for the reader knows more of the character than the character does of himself, yet the weaknesses, reasoning, and situations of the protagonist are directed at the reader in an aggressive fashion by the personal address implicit in the pronoun. Alternatively, Delmont, having decided at the end of his journey to write a book about his experience, could be dictating the story to himself as he writes: a conscious reconstruction of the flow of thought. The very possibility of multi-level interpretation jolts the reader into new awareness, preventing him from slipping into his old reading habits.

Degrés has relationships which are more complex because they shift.[18] The book is divided into three sections: in the first Pierre Vernier is writing in his own name (*je*) to his nephew Pierre Eller (*tu*) about the boy's world (*nous, vous, il, ils*). He introduces the pupils in Eller's class and their teachers in groups of three and intends to recount the whole school year. It proves impossible to deal with so many people and the ever increasing number of inter-connections between them, so in the second section Vernier restricts his description. He presents events through the eyes of his nephew; thus the *je-tu* relationship is reversed and complicated, for this part is ostensibly written by Eller (*je*) for Vernier (*tu*) but is in fact still written by Vernier. Hence the relationship shown is a false one. Vernier begins to lose his grasp and the third section of *Degrés* is written by another of Eller's uncles, Henri Jouret, who becomes in his turn *je*. Eller returns to his place as *tu* and Vernier is exiled to the third person. The second person chosen for Eller is the one discussed by Butor in "L'usage des pronoms personnels dans le roman," the *tu* used for didactic purposes to teach Eller something he did not know about his own life. It also includes the reader in the story, so that this relationship with the characters is perturbed when the pronouns are changed.

By his choice of pronouns the author creates relationships with his reader, with and between the characters, between the individuals and groups to which they belong. The pronoun must be interpreted "comme une fonction à l'intérieur d'un milieu mental et social, dans un espace de dialogue." (*Ed. M.*)[19] Society is made up of dialogues which new forms of language modify as much as any other social phenomenon does.[20] The novel must seize society from the inside in such a way that no one can escape from it. The language of a work

31

binds the reader and author to the world represented, for the act of writing supposes a reader, just as all spoken language is dialogue. The book then becomes the centre of a network of dialogues within it and radiating out from it for which it is a source of reference, just as the individual is the centre of a number of groups each of which he will influence and which will influence him in its turn.

For Butor, people and all the objects and forces around them form constantly changing patterns which he must transmit. He must therefore create some kind of polyphonic technique, inevitably non-chronologicial, which then leads to the need for mobile forms to contain the new ways of story-telling.

L'étude des propriétés visuelles de cet objet qu'est un livre permettra d'apporter à de tel problèmes des solutions toutes nouvelles qui non seulement ouvriront des perspectives immenses à l'art du roman mais mettront à la disposition de chacun de nous des instruments pour saisir le mouvement des groupes dont nous faisons partie.[21] (*Ed. M.*)

But not only the visual properties have this importance, the musical ones too, as we have seen already, are important to the structure and impact of a book. Butor develops this idea in "Notes sur le livre aujourd'hui" where he speaks of a constant dialogue between all works of art past and present, giving to music and the visual arts a formative influence over writing similar to that which Latin and Greek had on the French language in the Renaissance.

A book can conduct a dialogue within itself, with illustrations included in the text or with other works by means of reference only.

La volume peut répartir les tâches autour de lui et avoir toutes sortes de degrés d'indépendance.[22] (*Ed. M.*)

Such independence requires mobility of form. And inevitably we think of *Mobile* itself, Butor's first obviously innovative publication.

Le livre, tel que nous le connaissons aujourd'hui, c'est donc la disposition du fil du discours dans l'espace à trois dimensions selon un double module: longueur de la ligne, hauteur de la page, disposition qui a l'avantage de donner au lecteur une grande liberté de déplacement par rapport au "déroulement" du texte, une grande mobilité, qui est ce qui se rapproche le plus d'une présentation simultanée de toutes les parties d'un ouvrage.[23] (*Ed. M.*)

Given this arrangement, each double page presents itself as a visual diptych affecting the reader's attitude to the text it contains (Plate 4). The structure of the work can thus be made extremely clear on a level different from that of a text-lecture. The geographic distances, repetitions and similarities of the USA are shown by the use of three margin widths, various typefaces and layout of *Mobile*. The book offers a catalogue of the country and thus is established in alphabetical sections. The reader may select any area he wishes to look at, choose many varied itineraries through the country and the book or use the text as a work of reference. The divisions are as clear as those offered by a grid system laid upon a map.

Description de San Marco uses similar typography to distinguish between levels of understanding (Plate 5). Butor explains that as the major portion of the basilica is Byzantine, the text has to preserve the symmetry of the style. The paragraphs are set in perfect rectangles and the number of lines in each is part of the pattern of the work as a whole. A forward thrust through time is produced as a result because some of the paragraphs necessarily end in mid-sentence, a sentence taken up again several paragraphs or even pages later. This book is divided into the same sections as the building it describes and hence the reader may again choose his own pathway through it.

6 810 000 litres d'eau par seconde has a different mobility. Prepared as a text for stereophonic radio it has, as numerous parentheses, scenes which can or need not be played, so that the work can become a play of almost any length according to the route chosen. (Several are indicated by the author.) As the text is stereophonic the voices destined to emerge from each speaker are printed in blocks on either side of the page. The reader must select which he will read first — a decision which colours his impression of the book and which produces a different effect from its audition. Then the voices are heard simultaneously, producing clashes of words which have a poetic or humorous effect difficult to establish from the written page alone. The listener has the added freedom of being able to adjust his radio in such a way that certain of the voices are lost at a given moment or others dominate throughout.

Butor's text of *Litanie d'eau*, first published with a series of engravings by G. Masurovsky,[24] follows the movements of the water itself (Plates 6 and 7). Butor compares it to a musical score — dialogue is again on various levels.

J'ai écrit en des strophes de même format [que celui des phénomènes dans les eaux-fortes] une sorte de discours de l'eau sur elle-même, avec une grammaire telle que les mots y fussent comme des gouttes emportées dans diverses houles. Lorsque j'ai dû séparer ces strophes des images, je les ai placées au bas des pages comme une base architecturale, ou une basse. Dans la partie supérieure j'ai inscrit quelques mots, comme des "traits" se superposant à cette note fondamentale. Imaginez un accord épais, évoluant lentement, et par dessus, des trilles.[25]

Other texts prepared with artists were printed on loose leaves so that the reader can arrange them as he will. Verses of *La Chanson de Don Juan*[26] are flexible within the grammatical constructions themselves. Each stanza contains thirty grammatical entities forming the description of a woman (Shakespearean name, place of origin, etc.) and these stanzas are written on each side of twenty cards. Each card has a certain number of holes in it, giving grammatical blanks of one, two, three and four units respectively. Thus by changing the order of the cards and hence the attributes of the ladies, eight hundred different women are available immediately. The reader may increase this number indefinitely by changing some of the adjectives himself. Another work of multiple significance is *La Querelle des Etats* prepared with Camille Bryen.[27] This work combines texts drawn from Perrault's stories with various states of a three-stage engraving; these elements combine with the title to give assorted possible meanings (Plates 8 and 9).

Butor sees books as objects in a world of objects and constantly explores ways in which they can be made more influential. He studies every aspect of form and content to see the role each plays in the accuracy of the final expression. He quotes Hugo as saying that the book is a form of architecture freed from its site (having previously stated for himself that "toute architecture, toute organisation d'un site, est déjà une écriture élémentaire").[28] (*Ed. M.*) Like sites, literature acts on the space around man in the present, preserves a transcription of the past and prepares a future that will be written down in its turn.

Le livre nous permet de vaincre le temps, mais aussi l'espace; c'est en grande partie par l'intermédiaire des livres que nous sommes en communication et le téléphone implique son annuaire.[29] (*Ed. M.*)

Butor believes that the role of the book is being transformed at the present time and that it merits attention and skilled work for the book is the score of civilization. It is the job of the critic to recognize the books which are valuable to his time and to make them known to the public. This way his work becomes part of a chain of discovery as surely as does that of any other creative writer, for it remains as a work of reference and a possible means of access to a new world.

34

WORKSHEETS FOR *BOOMERANG*

Worksheets for *Boomerang*, showing how Butor plans the intricate integration of elements in his works.

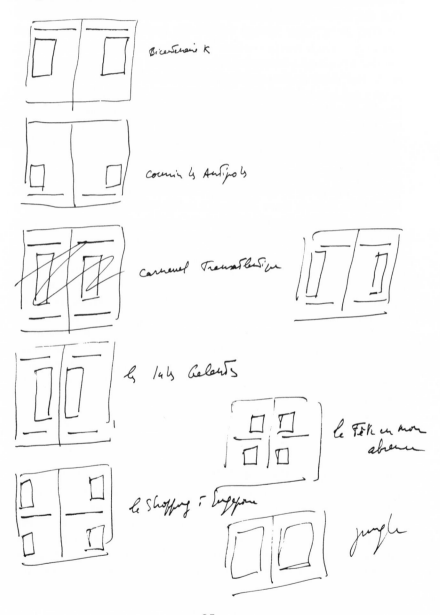

36

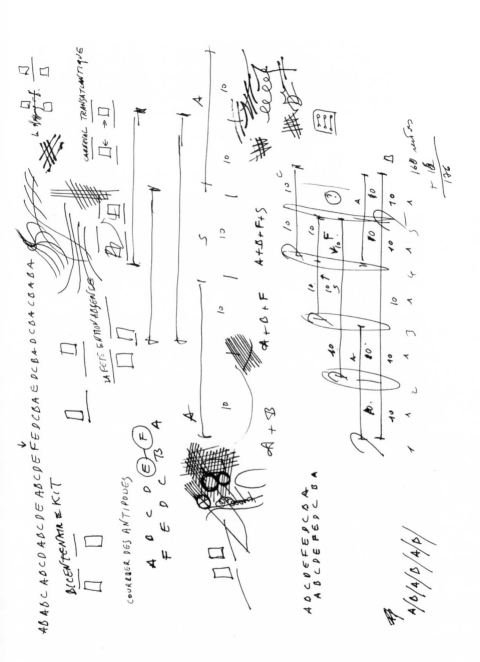

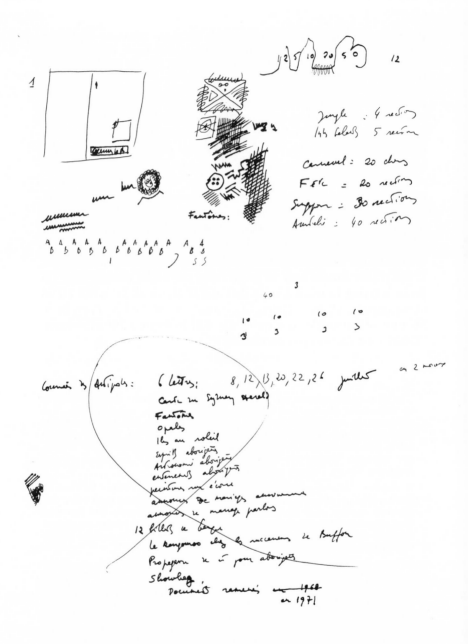

Restitution du texte ancien, invention du texte nouveau sont deux actions corrélatives. Plus je restitue, plus je suis forcé d'inventer (et encouragé dans cette aventure) ; plus j'invente, plus je suis capable de restituer.[30] (*Ed. M.*)

Awareness in analysis brings skill in construction; care in reading produces craftsmanship in writing; study develops the imagination which when exercised improves understanding. Butor's critical work thus supports his fiction; his own attitude towards his own work brings the literature of the past into question and gives it a new life closely applicable to the present situation. "La marque même d'une profonde nouveauté, c'est son pouvoir rétroactif."[31]

Butor sees literature as the key to a network of communication stretching across the whole history of man and enveloping the entire globe. Within it lies all available knowledge, all the discoveries and dreams of the human situation, and from it the future will be built. If the reader knows how to profit from the books around him (as Butor is trying to teach him to do) and if above all he is not afraid of complexity, all the richness of civilization can be his. Then he in his turn will struggle to acquire the skill to express his experience. "Ecrire c'est l'action par excellence."[32]

CHAPTER II: FOOTNOTES

[1] The ideas in this chapter are drawn for the most part from: the three volumes of *Répertoire* (Paris: Les Editions de Minuit, 1960, 1964, 1968) ; "Les tendances du roman français après la dernière guerre," *NM (Neusprachliche Mitteilungen aus Wissenschaft und Praxis)* 4 (1966), pp. 193-207; "Notes sur le livre aujourd'hui," *Kentucky Romance Quarterly*, XVIII, 2 (1971), pp. 133-144; "Propos sur l'écriture et le typographie," *Communication et Langages*, No. 13 (March 1972), pp. 5-29.

[2] R. Barthes, "Littérature et Discontinu," *Essais Critiques* (Paris: Editions du Seuil, 1964), p. 186: "It is by testing scraps of events against each other that meaning appears, it is by tirelessly transforming those events into functions that structure is built: Like the handyman, the writer (poet, novelist or essayist) only *sees* the meaning of the inert units which are in front of him when he relates them."

[3] P. 154: "it is only when things get complicated that they begin to appear clearly."

[4] "Le Roman comme recherche," p. 10: "I call 'symbolism' of a novel all the relations between what it describes and the reality in which we live. These relations are not the same from novel to novel and it seems to me that the essential task of the critic is to sort them out, throw light on them so that everything a particular work has to teach can be extracted from it.... The novel's external symbolism tends to be reflected in an internal symbolism, parts of which play in relation to the whole the role the work has in relation to reality."

5 "Le Roman et la poésie," *Répertoire II*, p. 25: "The novelist is he who notices that a structure is taking shape in his environment, and who will follow up the structure, make it grow, perfect it, study it until it becomes legible to everyone."

6 "Influences de formes musicales sur quelques oeuvres," *Musique en jeu*, No. 4 (Paris: Editions du Seuil, 1972), p. 65.

7 *Répertoire II*, p. 42: "In the last few years critics have begun to realise the special value of the novelist's work in the exploration of the dimension of time, the close relationship between this art and another which is created above all within time: music. Beyond a certain level of reflection one cannot help but see that most musical problems have corresponding ones in the novel and that music structures can be applied to the novel. . . . Music and the novel throw light on each other."

8 "Le Roman et la poésie," p. 23: "If we are capable of joining them to each other [everyday sentences] inside strong forms, these sentences, which seem so banal at first sight, show that they have a significance we had forgotten or had not known how to hear."

9 J. Ricardou, "Temps de la narration, temps de la fiction," *Problèmes du nouveau roman* (Paris: Editions du Seuil, 1967) gives a detailed analysis of this aspect of *L'Emploi du Temps*.

10 "La Répétition" and "Une Possibilité", *Répertoire*, pp. 94-109, 110-114.

11 A murder upsets the natural order. The detective sets out to work through the evidence in order to arrive at the truth, the revelation of which is, in effect, a second murder re-establishing an equilibrium. However, as the detective is born of the criminal's action, he is in the position of Oedipus — he kills his father. (The situation of Theseus in the tapestry and the relationship between Burton and Revel are of the same order.) Also the detective is working in two time sequences: one moves forward towards understanding, the other back towards the unknown action and the two are totally interdependent. See *L'Emploi du Temps* pp. 146-148, 161, 171, 174.

12 For a study of *La Modification* and *Degrés* see J. Roudaut, "Répétition et modification dans deux romans de Michel Butor," *Saggi e ricerche di letteratura francese*, VIII (1967), pp. 309-364.

13 *Les Lettres Nouvelles* (December 1960); *L'Arc*, No. 6 (Spring 1959); *Illustrations*, pp. 56-77, 93-105; *Cahiers du Chemin*, No. 13 (1971), p. 47

14 "L'Espace du roman," *Répertoire II*, p. 44: "All fiction is registered in our space as a journey . . . any novel that tells the story of a journey is therefore clearer, more explicit than one which cannot express metaphorically this distance between the place where the reading is taking place and the one the story leads us to."

15 Interview with Claude Couffon, *Les Lettres Françaises* (19 December 1963): "What interests me above all now is to try and make objects speak for themselves, to force objects into speech. If they are arranged in a certain way that produces sparks."

16 *Le Figaro Littéraire* (7 December 1957): "It was absolutely necessary to tell the story from the point of view of a character. As it was a question of his becoming aware, it was not possible that the character should say *I*. I had to have an interior monologue beneath the level of the language of the character himself, in a form between the first and third persons. This *you* allows me to describe the situation of the character and the way language is born in him."

17 Françoise van Rossum-Guyon, *Critique du Roman* (Paris: Gallimard, 1970), pp. 114-174.

18 J. Roudaut, *Michel Butor ou le livre futur* (Paris: Gallimard, 1964), pp. 92-97.

19 "L'Usage des pronoms personnels dans le roman," *Répertoire* II, p. 72: "as a function inside a mental and social milieu, within a space of dialogue."

20 "Notes sur le livre aujourd'hui," *Kentucky Romance Quarterly*, XVIII, 2 (1971), pp. 135-136.

21 "Individu et groupe dans le roman," *Répertoire II*, p. 87: "The study of the visual properties of the object which is a book will allow one to bring to such problems brand new solutions which will not only open immense horizons to the art of the novel but will put at the disposal of each of us instruments for grasping the movement of the groups we are part of."

22 *Ibid.*, p. 142: "The novel can spread its tasks around itself and achieve all kinds of degrees of independence."

23 "Le Livre comme objet," *Répertoire II*, p. 107: "The book as we know it today is the disposition of the thread of speech in three dimensional space according to a double measure: length of line, height of page, an arrangement which has the advantage of giving the reader greater freedom of movement in reaction to the 'unfolding' of the text, great mobility which is the nearest thing to the simultaneous presentation of all parts of a work."

24 Reprinted in *Illustrations* (Paris: Gallimard, 1964), pp. 107-188.

25 "Influences de formes musicales sur quelques oeuvres," *Musique en jeu*, No. 4 (Paris: Editions du Seuil, 1972), p. 69: "I wrote in stanzas of the same format as those of the phenomena in the engravings, a sort of monologue of the water about itself, with a grammar which made the words seem like drops carried by various swells. When I had to separate the stanzas from the images, I put them at the bottom of the pages like an architectural base or a musical bass. In the upper part I wrote a few words like "runs" superimposed on the original note. Imagine a heavy chord evolving slowly and trills on top of it."

26 Explained by Butor, 13th August 1972 at St Laurent-du-Var. Examples and explanation in *Degrés*, No. 1 (Brussels, January 1973).

27 Les Editions Brunidor (Paris 1973).

28 "La littérature, l'oreille et l'oeil," *Répertoire III*, p. 402 and p. 392: "all architecture, all organization of a site is already an elementary form of writing."

29 *Ibid.*, p. 403: "The book allows us to conquer time, but also space; it is mainly by the intermediary of books that we are in communication and the telephone implies the directory."

30 "La critique et l'invention," *Répertoire III*, p. 13: "Reconstitution of an old text, invention of a new one, are two inter-related actions. The more I reconstitute, the more I have to invent (and encouraged in this adventure), the more I invent, the more I am capable of reconstituting."

31 *Ibid.*, p. 13: "The true mark of a real innovation is its retroactive power."

32 "Notes sur le livre aujourd'hui," p. 136: "Writing is the supreme action."

CHAPTER III

Sites

Michel Butor has always been sensitive to the power exerted by his environment. The very title of the collection of his early poems, *La banlieue de l'aube à l'aurore*, shows an awareness of its changing aspects and the attention paid to every nuance of its transformations. Butor himself and all his fictional characters are tied tightly to their surroundings; if we look at the sites he chooses to present and the way he describes them, by and large in the order in which the works were published, it should be possible to see the role environment plays in the author's concept of his world.

Passage de Milan transmits the idea of a social space. The building with which the novel is concerned contains a complete schema of Parisian society, each inhabitant being representative of a certain section of the population. The bounds of this society become the outer walls of the building from which Louis Lécuyer is finally expelled and from outside of which come Ahmed and Henri Delétang. Class distinctions and differences of race and creed which divide people into small groups are shown as solid divisions within the building. They are the walls which create small cells within the large structure. The cell-structure is stable because everyone belongs to a major ethnic, religious or social group although they circulate between this centre and a number of other groups to which they belong by profession, interest or inclination.

Butor is extremely conscious of this structure. It is a perpetual reminder of the conditions and limitations of daily life, even a phenomenological description of them. The same walls run down through all the levels of the building, but the compartments they enclose, though parallel, differ in occupant, decoration and use according to their relative position in the microcosm. The walls conduct sound through the block very much in the way that the divisions in society are the bearers of gossip and rumour. It is significant that these noises can be heard most clearly at the hours when people are taking their leisure and can pay attention to them.

There are two staircases in the building, one of which serves the main entrance to each apartment, the other the kitchen door; these staircases are separated by a simple pane of glass (accident of birth?) and give equal possibility of climbing up through the building, though the front doors are, of course, served by an elevator also. The back stairs go up to the attics and down to the cellars — parts of the house which remain unvisited by its respectable inhabitants, but which are nonetheless essential to the functioning of the amenities enjoyed at the other levels. The sixth floor represents the fringe respectability of the working class and student population which supplies the man-power for the rest of the building, while the cellar is the centre for the basic mechanical necessities: water, electricity, transport. The foundations of the building are on top of an old church, giving the community a symbolic base, and it is from here that destiny seems to direct events. Henri Delétang hides in the cellar before returning to the Vertigues' flat; Louis Lécuyer finds refuge there immediately after the accident and it is there that Samuel Léonard comes to rescue him. It is the home of guilt, sin and wretchedness — ideas underlying the whole of Judeo-Christian society. In complete contrast to the cellar is the roof which can also be reached from the back stairs only. Félix Mogne goes there in his dream and Louis Lécuyer is there, dreaming of Angèle when he hears her cry out.

Each floor of the building represents a different class of society and the most successful is deep in its heart. This is the rich Jewish household headed by Samuel Léonard from which emerges the Egyptian influence which pervades the house and all discussion on literary presentation of society. The third floor is enclosed by the apartment of the Vertigues, an upper-middle class pretentious family on the floor above, and the numerous family of a bureaucrat below on the second floor. Continuing to work outwards we find on the edges of society priests on the first floor, artists on the fifth. As stated above the working class occupies the ground floor and the sixth, and people who have no regular place in the system are to be found on the roof or in the cellar. The cellar, because of its proximity to the church, provides a rebel (a forerunner of Cain) in the shape of Henri Delétang and a seeker of refuge in Louis. (We remember that it is Léonard himself who comes to look for Louis, provoking an inevitable comparison with both the prophet Samuel and Daniel in the lions' den.)

The apartment building in *Passage de Milan* is thus seen to incorporate the various elements of society and illustrate the interrelations within and between groups, each of which has its own rules and rituals and maintains its own facade. Any happening is seen to provoke a modification of the entire structure (Jean Ralon establishes this at the beginning of the novel when he reflects on the changing aspect of the open space outside his window — an excellent example of the internal symbolism of the book reflecting its external significance). The atmosphere is one of instability and profound though dissimulated malaise.

Here we have Butor's definition of a situation within which many of his readers find themselves and it provides at the same time a primary definition of a site as a socio-historical complex in a given geographical position. The building in *Passage de Milan* is built on Christian foundations but the beliefs and practices of its inhabitants are profoundly influenced by an earlier history, that of Egypt, as indeed the very title of the book indicates, for the *milan* (kite) is the sacred bird of Horus and it flies over the house.

The house is therefore the basic site which influences us all, and close behind it in importance comes the town, to which the author introduces us in *L'Emploi du Temps*. Bleston dominates the novel with a malefic force destined to subjugate its residents. As presented by Revel, the town is a narrow, gloomy representation of the English industrial north where Butor himself spent two unhappy years.[1] The town and its society are seen from the outside by a foreigner who does not understand the customs of the city and has access to few of its homes. The very fact that Revel does not speak English is an indication of his state of mind.

The city is populated by the usual mixture of foreigners and natives to be found in any industrial area in Britain. As the most important characters in the novel are Horace Buck, Revel and their friends, the book forms on a superficial level a criticism of Britain as seen by foreigners. Local inhabitants divide into groups according to work, interests or religious persuasion. Indifferent or repressed, they tend not to be open to new ideas or to people whose ways are strange to them. The only homes into which Revel is welcomed belong to exceptional members of the community: Buck who is a stranger too, Jenkins who being closely involved with unusual ways of thought (New Cathedral, detective stories) is more tolerant than

44

the majority of his neighbours, the Baileys who share his religious traditions and whose daughter Rose speaks his language (Anne also sells him the map of Bleston) and the Burtons. George Burton and his wife are authors and help him to understand the town in which they are to a certain extent exiles too.

The atmosphere in Bleston is oppressive, the people herd together in large crowds to spend their leisure hours, there is no sign of culture (except in the existence of a university) nor desire for individuality of thought or expression. The persons who differ in their beliefs from the ordinary citizens are ostracized or victimized for their points of disagreement even if their habits conform for the most part to those of the mass.

The mechanical functions necessary to the town make far more impression on Revel than the movement of its citizens because the former have a direct influence on his own life. Routine and structured systems like the public transport thus give form to the town and dominate human behaviour. From time to time a Bleston inhabitant rouses himself from his daily round to make a symbolic gesture of revolt, but this has little effect and both activator and crime seem to fade from public view. In fact, of course, the perturbation does not disappear: Tenn's murder is denounced by Burton and his book is an encouragement to Revel and hence to Buck.

Revel, a stranger arriving in such a town, finds its atmosphere overpowering: newness of routine, darkness of the building, inclemency of the climate, lack of friends, inability to communicate even if the people should prove willing to welcome him, which on the whole they do not. Add to these conditions depressing, cramped lodgings and it is not surprising that the newcomer should feel that the town is possessed of a malevolent force:

Cet air auquel j'étais désormais condamné pour tout un an ... j'ai bien senti qu'il contenait des vapeurs sournoises ... qui avaient réussi à me plonger dans le terrible engourdissement dont je viens de me réveiller.[2] (*Ed. M.*)

(Revel's hotel is called "The Screw" — a reminder perhaps of Henry James' novel *The Turn of the Screw* which treats of a stranger's struggle to break evil forces at work in a house.)

Here for the first time Butor's protagonist is obliged to find his way in an unknown environment. The building in *Passage de Milan* provided bounds within which the intricacies of a known environment were confined. It had no specific past and the disruption of

45

its order came from outside. Bleston is sufficient unto itself. Everything that happens is the inexorable product of its own structure and history. It seems to be all-embracing and inescapable and for this reason certain of the characters fear and fight its powers. Jenkins, who has spent all his life in Bleston, is as conscious of the force of the town as Revel is (pp. 91-92). These few people have to understand what is going on around them in order to survive, for it is not possible to escape by any means other than the achievement of total comprehension.

To understand a city one must find and understand its centres. These are indicated by signs within the city itself for those who know how to find them. In Bleston the buses offer the key: the ones with numbers prefixed 1 start from the Old Cathedral, those prefixed 2 from the Town Hall and 3 from the railway stations in Alexandra Square. The stations obviously provide the point of entry into the town and are symbols of the links with the outside world. The Town Hall is its administrative hub and the Old Cathedral the centre of its beliefs; hence the first site to be studied must be the Old Cathedral. This is a Roman Catholic edifice in Gothic style which is known for a series of stained glass windows descriptive of the old order: above the altar Christ sat in judgment, on His right were scenes from the life of Abel and pictures of all the righteous cities, and on His left Cain, Sodom, Babylon and Imperial Rome. All had been destroyed in the course of time except for the panel of Cain. The importance of this is made clear to Revel by a book he buys because it is called *Le Meurtre de Bleston*, by an author called J-C Hamilton. This becomes his manual and guide for it teaches him to read his environment, hence indicating Butor's own intention in his detailed descriptions of Bleston in *L'Emploi du Temps*.

Cain's fratricide is given its full symbolic importance in *Le Meurtre de Bleston* (Bleston's Murder) and Revel recognizes that Bleston prison on his map is the same shape as the mark on Cain's forehead. In the background of the Cain window in the cathedral is a city in flames and its gates, topped by the crescent of the infidel, are identical to those of Plaisance Gardens, the chief amusement park in Bleston. J-C Hamilton's book directs Revel to the Old Cathedral, Horace Buck takes him to Plaisance Gardens where he meets George Burton, the author who used J-C Hamilton as a pseudonym. The division in Revel and in Burton is one which divides the town itself and is forever reflected in the scene of dissension between Cain and Abel. Plaisance Gardens leads Revel on to

46

explore the patches of waste ground around the town where the fair can be found on a yearly circuit of the city and also to the Amusement Arcade in the middle of Bleston where Buck and Revel spend Christmas Day — both the place and time of the first fire to break out in Bleston. As foretold in the Cain window there continues to be fires in the fairground and amusement parks throughout Revel's stay. The fairgrounds are counterbalanced by a large number of parks dotted around Bleston and the Plaisance Gardens are likewise balanced by the Old Cathedral.

Interest in the Old Cathedral leads naturally to interest in the New Cathedral which stands not far from its predecessor. Built to rehouse the bells for which the town was famous (Butor gives the etymology Bells Town-Bleston) at a time when the structure of the Old Cathedral became too weak to support them, it indicates a shift of belief for the bells called the people to worship. The move was not very great, however, as the New Cathedral was also built in the Gothic style. Gothic architecture is the physical manifestation of medieval belief; firmly planted on earth, its structural lines indicating its heavenly aspirations, it is covered with angels, saints, men, beasts and devils representing the chain of being on which the eternal hierarchy depended. By being constructed in the old style the New Cathedral reinforced belief in the basic structure of the world but its decoration indicates a new outlook. Dominated by the Cross of the New Testament rather than the prohibitions and punishments of the Old, the New Cathedral contains representations of every species of the natural world from the simplest mollusc to the races of man — and the human beings are in the chapel, in the most important position. Scientific reason has supplanted heavenly rule. (It is ironic that Jenkins should remark that the statues of human types are the least successful of the carvings.)

George Burton's book led Revel to the Cathedrals, but Burton cannot guide Revel any further as is shown in his alias J-C Hamilton: J-C links him to Christ, Hamilton binds him to his geographical area, so that he cannot escape from the town or its values. In his explanation of the form of the detective story[3] he shows how every new development is achieved through death and rebirth. Each person strives to discover the cause of the death before and then must die himself. Bernard Winn was killed in the Old Cathedral, after killing his brother Johnny in the new one. Revel must work through the cycle for himself and go beyond his mentor. This is shown clearly in his dream where he huddles in the shadow of the crucifix while the New Cathedral grows and grows around him. Jenkins helps him a little but is impeded by his hatred of Burton just as Buck is impeded by his hatred of Bleston itself.

Butor's lesson is clear: people and books can be of great assistance, but finally the relationship between a person and his environment is an intimate one for him alone. Bleston provides a description of the complexity of the world and Revel is grappling with the basic problems posed by modern society. In an interview[4] Butor once expressed the view that a town or a monument is as much a work of art as a painting, but being a collective one it is much more difficult to analyse as there are many more levels to study. Butor has created a town to show his reader how to analyse the real ones around him. Bleston is a complex structure with many possible levels of significance. These will create effects which differ from reader to reader according to his knowledge and experience. They are presented in a didactic fashion here; the buildings, the book, the other symbolic objects are offered in a way that demands interpretation and the astute reader will use the Theseus tapestries in the museum to shed light on Revel's behaviour even before indication is given that he should. Just as Theseus' father recognizes his son by his sword and later dies as a result of Theseus' thoughtlessness, so Burton meets Revel because the latter has a copy of *Le Meurtre de Bleston* and then has an accident because Revel crumpled the negative of a photograph of Burton and his wife and also revealed the identity of J-C Hamilton to Anne and Rose. Bleston becomes the Minotaur, and the labyrinth, as in mediaeval literature, is the thread of man's life on earth. Each man must conquer his environment or become absorbed by it as have many of Revel's colleagues who bear names of local importance. Ardwick, the name of one of the clerks at Matthews and Son, is also the name of an area of Manchester, Dalton is a town in Lancashire and also one in Northumberland, Blyth(e) is also in Northumberland (but could also be an ironic reflection on the man's character). There is a Moseley street in Manchester, and Slade Hall is the name of a sixteenth century house on its outskirts. Greystone is probably a comment on the industrial cities. Either way man is indissolubly bound to a site both as its product and as a moment in its existence.

Although Revel's position in Bleston is a complicated one it is by no means the culmination of Butor's expression of man's position. Cities do not stand alone. They stand in direct geographical, historical and ideological relation to others (just as people collect in

48

groups). This Butor discusses in an essay about the network of temples spread over Ancient Greece.[5] Each was born of the need for the god, in a site made for the god and which gave the god his rightful position among the others in his area; thus a pilgrim standing within one temple could see and feel the lines joining him to many others. A polytheist cannot trust in one single power any more than a modern man can spend his life sufficient unto himself within one site. The young Butor in *Portrait de l'artiste en jeune singe* was contained within the walls of H (Harburg) until he had assimilated all the castle had to teach him; for a time he was H, but then he outgrew its limits and moved on to Egypt.

Similarly, Léon Delmont (*La Modification*) is identified with his environment; he is the train which contains so many possible facets of himself and which travels between his wife Henriette and his mistress Cécile in the two cities they reflect for him. Hence he is torn between two poles of a greater complexity than Revel's. Travelling through the countryside which separates Paris and Rome, Delmont's memories linger in each of the cities in turn as his stream of thought evolves. These cities have a tremendous importance in the formation of the final decision for his future. All the cultural, historical and artistic power associated with them is used by Butor to create the atmosphere and background necessary to stimulate Delmont's feelings and show the reasons for his reactions and relationships. This time Butor has chosen to use real cities, and so more complex elements are brought into the book by the unexpected provided by the cities themselves and by the reader. Familiarity with Rome in particular gives extra depth to the possible interpretation of the novel. The author is drawing on knowledge his reader may have amassed from other sources, so that every interpretation of the book will be coloured by subjective considerations or weakened by a lack of them. No standard version of this story can be accepted as having incorporated every possible level of meaning.

Rome dominates the work with Paris in its shadow. The important parts of Paris for Delmont are the ones which recall Rome: the Baths of Julian the Apostate on Boulevard St Michel because they are genuinely Roman, the Panthéon for its style and spirit. Delmont lives beside the Panthéon and can admire its freize from his home. The Avenue de l'Opéra is where he works for his Roman employers and the travel agency next door to his office has posters showing different regions all the way to Rome and on to Sicily: a daily reminder of his journey to Cécile and an indication that it is possible

49

to go beyond her, to find roots deeper than Rome. Nearby is a Roman Bar. The Louvre is mentioned for Pannini's cityscapes of Imperial and Renaissance Rome; a concept of the parallels and differences between these two periods is essential for an understanding of Delmont's position, but by tracing them in Paris Delmont is distorting and underestimating the value of his hometown. He must let it speak for itself.

Ancient Rome was pagan and it is among its relics that Léon is happiest, both on his honeymoon with Henriette and later walking with Cécile. For him this period symbolizes youth, freedom from responsibility and all the ideals attached to this, ideals which he has tried to recapture in his relationship with Cécile. Pictures of the monuments, gifts from his mistress, hang in his Paris home, there recalling both his present love for Cécile and the happy moments on which his marriage is based. That he lives near to the Panthéon would suggest that he has in his possession the best possible combination of idealism and daily routine, but instead of living happily beside the monument he uses it to build up nostalgia for an earlier, purer ideal. He refuses to accept Paris as it is and insists on considering it a pale version of Rome — hence in his view his wife loses in comparison with Cécile.

Delmont identifies himself with Rome at the height of its power, in the early days of Christianity. He refuses to accept that he is rather the reflection of the Rome of Leo X, when the Church was all powerful in the city, opulent and tormented, mature and rift by schism. Baroque architecture is the struggle expressed in visual form. Delmont visits all the works of the major artists of the period: Bernini, Borromini and above all Michelangelo. Here Rome gives us the key to Delmont's life. The centre of Renaissance Rome is the Sistine Chapel. In it are united the pagan and Christian worlds in all their wisdom, sibyls and prophets together. This is the place where the idealistic and the realistic can be synthesized into one magnificent whole, where the Christian present manifests its pagan origins and the legitimate development from one to the other is obvious. The best of both ways of thought are joined, giving added power to each.

Henriette tends to be identified with religion devoid of art, with Roman Catholicism and the Vatican and so with a set of values which, though excellent in themselves, have become rigid and out of touch with the modern world. Cécile on the other hand visits only those works of Michelangelo which can be found outside the Vatican. Such a study lacks a knowledge of the edifice for which the artist's paintings were designed and is a view of the less comprehensive applications of his genius. Each creation stands alone like a single thought which does not form part of a philosophy. Both of the women are mistaken in their attitude. Cécile rejects anything which smacks of the established system within the Church while Henriette clings to the traditional structure and ignores everything outside it — at least in her husband's opinion. However, Henriette did visit the Sistine Chapel with her husband on their honeymoon, so it is possible that they may achieve a similar balance again.

The Chapel is undeniably a Christian work and so firmly represents stable social values, but incorporated into it are enough pagan elements to provide a continual harmony and stimulus. That Léon plans to revisit the Vatican during his weekend in Rome is symbolic of his decision to accept his responsibilities as well as to preserve a flexibility of outlook and some of his old ideals.

Delmont identifies with Rome and rejects Paris, but the cities have a clear relationship to one another which is measured by the train journeying between them. They are a specific distance apart and certain steps must perforce be accomplished in order to move from one to the other. Each journey must imply an equivalent mental development. *La Modification* shows even more clearly than *L'Emploi du Temps* the close identification in Butor's work between character and his world, and the way in which a lack of comprehension or information, or an over-subjective attitude, can impede the establishment of a healthy rapport between them. Delmont finds a historic parallel in the career of Julian the Apostate whose letters he reads. Like Julian he tries to reverse the advance of change by returning to a pagan Roman Empire, and like Julian he fails.

Looking back over *L'Emploi du Temps* and *La Modification* we realize how important it is for the character (and hence for Butor) to understand his past and the history of his environment in order to gain a grasp on the present and take decisions for the future. The perpetual impediment to such a course is the pressure of time which pushes the character forward, continually confronting him with new events long before he has been able to discover sufficient information about the preceding ones to be sure of their significance. *La Modification* is a control experiment in this as the pressures are on the train and not on Delmont himself, except in so far as we identify them with one another.

Having taught his reader how to look at a given environment in

L'Emploi du Temps by creating Bleston for that purpose and putting a character called Revel (reveal) inside it, Butor confronts his reader with real cities, Paris and Rome, carefully pointing the way he should go in order to build his own idea of Delmont from his knowledge of the sites. Thus he will perhaps see the relationship between himself and his own town and look at his daily situation with a new eye. A site is after all a place of significance to the beholder and one from which neighbouring places can be seen more clearly.

The lesson on how to read an environment is resumed by Butor in his next novel *Degrés* (a lesson for which *Le Génie du Lieu*, published in the same year, provides concrete example for it is Butor's own view of a number of sites, cities and countries). We remember that Pierre Vernier teaches history and geography, that he begins the year with a lesson on Egypt with his youngest pupils, that the central point of his year's planning for Eller's class is Christopher Columbus' discovery of the New World, and that he reaches this latter topic, not directly, but by way of historical and literary experience plus an acute sense of the marvels of exploration through the notebooks of Marco Polo and the essays of Montaigne. His work is supported directly by that of his colleague Henri Jouret who teaches literature. Some of the books Jouret proposes to his classes are applied directly by the pupils to their view of the situation in which they find themselves, Jouret applies others and it is not difficult for the reader to complete the work.[6] As soon as we look at education as a training for the understanding of the world around us all the subjects taught fall into a coherent pattern. We learn the rudiments of the structure of the physical world, the development (social, political and individual) of mankind, man's means of communication and of self-expression. It remains then to apply this knowledge intelligently and consistently to our surroundings — and in this Butor's work gives us practice for he never provides solutions for his readers.

Degrés then provides us with a theory and *Le Génie du Lieu* shows us how Butor uses it for himself. We read his reaction to Cordoba, Mantua, Delphi and above all Egypt, with pleasure at his expressive writing, wonder at his historic and artistic sensitivity and delight in his constant exploration. Here are sites as they should be appreciated and we understand why they do and should haunt the present with their power. Egypt and Greece lie at the foundation of *Passage de Milan, L'Emploi du Temps, La Modification* and *Degrés* not only because Butor lived in each country and learned to love them, but because their history as expressed in their sites has force enough still to penetrate the official development to which a Frenchman's life is bound — that of the Roman Catholic Church.

To date we have seen that a study of man in his environment produces three relationships: place to place, place to person and person to person within the influence of a site. In four books published between 1962 and 1965 Michel Butor proceeds to examine each of these relationships individually.

Réseau Aérien deals in the abstract with transport and communication as indeed its title implies. It is a radio play (again in the title) whose characters are on ten aeroplanes somewhere on one of the two Paris-New Caledonia routes going to or from Orly. The main impression is that of the ease with which it is possible to go from place to place and also the number of opportunities missed by the travellers of visiting some of the major sites outside Europe. *Réseau Aérien* is an indication of the network of relations in time and space and the links between them which spread over the globe at all times, and which vary according to the perspective of each observer.

Mobile[7] is above all concerned with connections between places. It provides a detailed study of a small part of the area covered by *Réseau Aérien*, the description of one country, but it differs profoundly from *Le Génie du Lieu* in that we see no personal fascination in the presentation of the USA. In fact there are no characters to provide it and Butor speaks in his own person only once, in the centre of the book (p. 233). As objective as the book appears to be, however, by the listing of the states in alphabetical order we must remember that this in itself constitutes a cultural bias — many cultures do not have the equivalent of an alphabetical series — and also that the alphabet is used on the French names of the areas, so that they are offered in an order different from the one habitual to the Americans themselves. We have an outsider's point of view. Butor has chosen a system for representing the USA which is at the roots of their tradition but has put it into practice through his own culture which has a slightly different optic.

This basis of his structure is thus the list and it recurs at all levels in *Mobile*: lists of ice cream flavours, cars, colours, garages, as though the author were providing us with a catalogue of the country in which the catalogue plays such an important role — and of course there are references to Sears Roebuck. But lists, like sentences, are linear and hence too simple to transmit the complexities to be found within a country, so Butor exploits the visual properties of the

53

printed page. He sets up a network of cities across the USA by the use of place names which are repeated and by multiple margins. Hence in the state of Arkansas (pp. 11-13) we see:

Florence
Florence
Georgetown
Georgetown
Georgetown
La Grange
La Grange
(*Ed. G.*) (Plate 4)

The first margin is used for towns within the state with which the chapter is concerned (Arkansas), the second for towns in adjoining states (Texas, Oklahoma, Louisiana, Mississippi) and the third for those in states further away (New Mexico). The cities form knots in a fabric of inter-relations in which their repetition and juxtaposition create a basic pattern of reference and resonance. All geographical, anthropological and historical data gain significances, when tied into the pattern, which are much greater than any of them might have in isolation and which often produce unexpected insights into the nature of the wider context.

After we have read about the European settlers, their hopes in coming to a New World and their subsequent treatment of the Indians, the fact that *Mobile* opens in the town of Cordoba, (we remember *Le Génie du Lieu* with its description of the mosque and all the Arab tradition by the Christians) and closes in Eden, Superior and finally Buffalo, takes on a supreme irony which reflects back to the frequent descriptions of Freedomland, the modern American dream and contemporary treatment of the black population. The states of the deep south are joined by the refrain "For whites only . . . whites only . . . only." Indian reservations and the name of each tribe are mentioned without fail all over the country and quotations are given from the treaties made and from the writings of some of the prominent Indians of the past. No comment is made; the facts speak for themselves quite well enough.

The racial problem is an important part of the pattern Butor is weaving and so is that of religion. The Salem witch trials, the Mormons, Puritans, Quakers, and the Indian peyote cults all play their part together with the pious restaurant-haven of repose in Los Angeles.

54

The natural attributes of each state are listed (and the fact that National Parks are called "monuments" thus giving them the appearance of being man-made is duly noted) together with artists and their works and museum collections. An indication of the effect the author is intending to achieve is given by his comparison of *Mobile* with the quilts in the Vermont museum (p. 29). These are patchwork mosaics, counterpoint of fabrics, and many of them are didactic in the scenes they represent. Butor's book has a similar visual aspect with its play of various types and margins and also a similar result.

The characters in *Mobile* are the great men of American history: Jefferson, Penn, Franklin, Carnegie, Lincoln. Franklin is one of the major centres and the town of Franklin is to be found in the very middle of the book. These men too are shown in a different light by juxtaposition of letters and official writings. The men who wrote the American constitution and set the foundation of the American dream today are seen to be racist capitalists living in European style luxury. References to the Chicago International Exhibition in 1893 reinforce the importance of trade and a consumer society.

There is a great sense of urgency throughout *Mobile* which stems from the brevity of most of the extracts quoted and observations made. The cars flash past with a hurried greeting or a roar and the very aspect of the book is such that certain words catch the reader's eye as billboards would if he too were driving across the USA. He has the impression that he is getting the superficial view of a passing tourist. This is accentuated again by the structure of *Mobile*; each section of the book is devoted to one state and the reader spends one swift hour in each so that, although fifty hours are spent on the journey, he is constantly shifted from day to night. The mobility might well translate the European's idea of an American's relationship to his environment — places are alike because they have the same name, so that they are geographical references rather than distinct sites. They are differentiated however by their various situations in time and space which place each of them in a different relationship to the whole environment, just as we see historic events which may well be part of the same movement but which have produced very different reactions in different geographical surroundings. The structure of *Mobile* makes this very obvious. The book expresses a dichotomy between dream and fact, countryside and object, bigotry and belief, white and coloured people in the life of the USA. Judgment and criticism are inherent in the structure;

minor observations recur, collect and build within the reader almost unbeknown to himself. *Mobile* has the flexible conditioning ability of the site itself on its inhabitants. It is constructed like the art from which it takes its name (Calder in Philadelphia), all the minor parts move, inter-react and change their appearance but the formative parts are rigid and do not allow the basic relationships to change; so it appears to be Butor's USA. In *Mobile* the relations of places in time have been isolated and a means of expression found for them. The USA with its relatively short history, scarcity of major artistic achievement and clearcut issues is ideal for Butor's purpose.

For his study of the relations between people and a site he chooses the Basilica of St. Mark in Venice because it too has qualities which lend themselves to his task. St. Mark's has a triple form of communication by which to express its importance and character: its architecture, the pictures in its mosaics and the words of the biblical quotations which accompany them. The traditions to be expressed are threefold also, those of Byzantium, of Judaism and of Venice itself, forming a second Trinity at the roots of the city whose centre is the Basilica. St. Mark's is the product of rivalry, commerce and pillage at the crossroads of three worlds whose centres are Constantinople, Alexandria and Rome. Finally, for Butor himself, it is the meeting place of three arts, architecture, literature and music, and he dedicates his description to Stravinsky whose *Canticum Sacrum in honorem Sancti Marci nominis* was written to be played in the great church.

The form of the *Description de San Marco* is given by these threefold influences. Again we find three margins and three kinds of type, representative of three levels of communication which are again reflected in the position of the narrator (Plate 5). Italics and the first margin are used for snatches of conversation in many different languages spoken by the tourists who are at floor level. Roman type and the second margin indicate the comments of the author who, because of his study, has access to a gallery which runs midway between floor and roof, while the third margin divides the description of the construction of the building and decoration (usually on the ceiling) from the more personal comment. Capital letters are reserved for the Latin words from the Bible which are a structural part of the edifice — here indeed the word is the manifestation of God in the structure of His Church. The site and the text bring forth the Basilica which in its turn interprets both to the true observer. Man, his language and his environment are here inseparable.

56

We see two relationships to the building in the juxtaposition of the tourists and the author, and that of the reader provides the seemingly inevitable third. These connections are formulated in the pattern of languages within *Description de San Marco*. In Butor's previous books we have seen that lack of knowledge of a language is indicative of an alienation from its culture, and we are reminded of this early in the book when the author writes:

Ceux qui parlent le vénitien, ceux dont l'italien est la langue maternelle, ceux qui le parlent couramment, ceux qui l'apprennent, ceux qui savent très bien se débrouiller pour quelques jours, ceux qui préfèrent ne pas se risquer hors de leur propre langue.[8] (*Ed. G.*)

Here are the levels of St. Mark's truly measured. In *Description de San Marco*, however, this is simplified into those who speak modern foreign languages, those who can read Butor's explanations and those who can read Latin for themselves, that is those who have no interest in the site they are in, those who can learn to understand it and those who are well advanced in wisdom. (Latin and other dead languages, Old German in *Portrait* for example, symbolize knowledge which is no longer a usual part of man's intellectual baggage.) There is a further complication in the Latin of St. Mark's, however; it is abbreviated. Hence the observer's knowledge must be precise enough for him to be able to recognize the formulae and give them back their full significance.

Again we meet the religious problem that has cropped up throughout Butor's writing. In most books there has been a church or a priest who is of scant assistance to a character needing direction in his daily life. Until now it has seemed that it was the religion itself that was at fault, and the founding of St. Mark's would substantiate this; but faced by the multitudinous inter-relations of history it enfolds, we realize that whether we continue to practice Christianity or not we still have need of an intimate knowledge of the history and symbolism of the Church in order to understand the civilization of Western Europe and all parts of the world colonized by it in the past.[9] (Delmont could not sever his connections with Rome, but he had to see them in perspective, hence his dream.)

By means of the history of its own values and development, its constantly modified structure and decorations, and the interplay of quotation and illustration which results and provides a wealth of unexpected information for the acute observer with an eye for juxtaposition, St. Mark's teaches its own brand of Christianity.[10] Just as

57

the play of light on the mosaics varies all the time, emphasizing one detail and then another, so the direction in which the visitor walks around the building will modify his version of the stories depicted above and around him. Built to house the body of the saint who wrote his personal history of the beginnings of a religion which taught by stories and which enfolded everybody, the Basilica accepts its visitors into its multitude of characters and includes their stories among the ones it tells.

Butor calls it the church of the Pentecost because of the multitude of languages united within it, but perhaps, as he also implies, it is rather a new Babel set up by the pride of the Venetians as a challenge to all peoples,[11] for only the disciples had the gift of tongues and Butor has mentioned earlier the pride with which the city of Venice, itself born of the separation of clay from water, identifies with Adam at his creation and hence takes supremacy over all others (p. 31).

St. Mark's then, teeming with people, biblical, historic and alive today, with its mixture of prophets, saints, infidels, doges, students and tourists, is a microcosm of Venice itself. Based on a religion which it flaunts as its most beautiful attribute, it is built with the spoils of war, the riches from trading agreements, so that even its most sacred relics have been stolen, humiliated, lost and re-established over the ages. We can see a pattern which grows out from the *Palo d'oro*, to the Basilica, to Venice, and then expands into the history of the Roman Catholic Church and that of the whole of Western Europe. Always rich, always flexible, St. Mark's stands in the heart of its city, growing naturally from among the shops and harbour traffic, witness in its own origins to a deal as outrageous as any discussed in its shadow; a site inseparable from its connections with man.

The third relationship is that between people within a given environment and this Butor explores in a radio play, *6 810 000 litres d'eau par seconde*.[12] This books is concerned with Niagara Falls and forms a diptych with *Mobile* by showing a large sampling of the American people visiting their most famous site during the course of a year. Niagara is known as a honeymoon centre, with the result that people go there with a preconceived idea of its *raison d'être* although they have ceased to understand the profundity of the myth. Couples of all kinds, married or not, and lonely individuals come to profit from the air of sentiment that surrounds its name. Most of them are disillusioned, however, because they do not know how to

58

respond to the site. They see the flowers, the souvenir shops and the falls but do not realize the deeper significance beneath the sentimentality and tourism. They cannot see beyond their own preoccupations and are as far apart as the banks of the falls: different countries with different histories and viewpoints.

Butor expresses the primitive power of the environment through quotation of Chateaubriand's descriptions of it which can be heard at intervals behind the conversations of the characters in the same way as what he described hovers behind the presence of Niagara. And the appearance of the place tells its own myth quite clearly. On the surface Niagara Falls, N.Y., and Niagara Falls, Ont., are joined by a bridge, the appearance of which can be considered a symbol of the link between and within the couples who visit the towns. This is only the superficial interpretation, however, as indicated by the fragility of the bridges there. Rather it is the dual nature of the site reflected in the difference in attitude between the types of tourist with their natural divisions of age, colour and sex. A more important sign of the power of Niagara Falls is to be found in the history of the people who risked and in some cases lost their lives crossing the falls in one direction or the other. Here we have surely an initiation into the mysteries of life and death. Life flows by like the water and then it is gone. Only by a sort of conquest can it be understood — Chapter X is called "Le Styx".

The modern version of this initiation rite is described in Chapter IV, "le voile de la mariée" (the bride's veil), when visitors go under the falling water. First the tourist is separated from his companion, then he is reduced to anonymity and stripped of his possessions. He has to take off all his clothes and put on a sort of pyjama suit and an oilskin before climbing up behind the wall of water. It is a repeat of the age-old maturation process of a hero going through death and rebirth, yet for the tourists it lacks any real significance; they are curious, embarrassed, a little troubled at the strangeness of their garb, but that is all. In failing to feel the importance of the ritual, or of its completion in the boat trip across the river below the falls, they have shown themselves immune to the true influence of Niagara, and also as the title of the chapter indicates to the real sacrament of marriage as a rebirth into new life.

The structure of *6 810 000 litres d'eau* helps to give the impression of the site today to the reader and is in marked contrast to the nobility of Chateaubriand's prose as he describes it in another age. Each section has more characters than the one before, is situated

59

one month later in the year and encompasses one more hour within its length. These hours are marked by chimes so that the passage of time can never be forgotten. The result is that the tempo of *6 810 000 litres* increases as more and more people pass in the accelerated time of each section. The characters are identified alphabetically in types: A and B are newly married, C and D older, E and F black, G and H a middle-aged lady and a gigolo and so on through to Q, Michel Butor's alter ego, a French visiting professor at the University of Buffalo, so that although the actual people differ from scene to scene, their attitudes, prejudices, situation and concerns tend to be repetitive. Hence by the end of the play the characters have lost all identity and flow by like the river itself. Having no myth, no ritual, they have no separate self.

In Niagara, Butor sees an image which parallels the impression he gave of the USA in *Mobile*: that of a site unaware of its own past and hence of its own power, concerned only with superficialities in the personal realm as much as in the public and environmental. Niagara is a site with unrealized potential, very different from the one offered by St. Mark's in Venice. The New World juxtaposed to the old in this way is shown to be of less use to its inhabitants in terms of interpretation and enrichment of their surroundings because, perhaps as a result of their lack of historical awareness, the people themselves are not able to recognize and develop knots of significance in their culture, so their networks are meaningless. Nothing is further from the spirit of overlapping strengths drawn from the Greek temples than the repetition of place names in *Mobile*.

For six years after the publication of *6 810 000 litres d'eau par seconde* Butor wrote nothing directly concerned with his environment, though the preface "Sites" was republished in *Répertoire III* and he worked on *Western Duo* (lithographs and text on the American Southwest) with G. Masurovsky, and wrote the *Quatre Lettres écrites du Nouveau Mexique à Camille Bryen*. The geographical movement of the author's interest was thus indicated but nothing foretold the synthesis forthcoming in *Où*.

Until *Western Duo* and the New Mexican lettres Butor had not directly expressed the sentiment he has for his environment since *Le Génie du Lieu*. *Où* is subtitled "Le Génie du Lieu II' and in it the author writes about his travels in his own person. In *Où* all the influences implied in the descriptions of the sites discussed above are brought together to show Butor's own development which is formed by the countries he has visited and reflected in his description of them. This development follows the one chosen by Vernier (*Degrés*) in his teaching ten years before. Butor moves from Paris, which continues to hold firm as one pole of his existence, through Egypt, though this time he does not stop there, and moves on to the Far East through Japan to Korea, whose monuments are but a step on the way to Cambodia and Angkor. The journey does not end there either, however; just as Vernier introduced his pupils to the New World by means of Marco Polo's writings on China so Butor travels on into the west of the USA, to Santa Barbara and finally to New Mexico which proves to be the other pole of attraction at this time.

The relative importance of each site is shown both in the length of its description and also in the influence it has on neighbouring sites (the descriptions are fragmented and intertwined) and the climatic element which controls it.[13] Throughout Butor's writing the land of Egypt has been synonymous with mystery, the alchemists and their experiments on metallic ore, the very foundations of knowledge, and therefore with earth. Korea is shown as the next step by the domination of an inter-element: mud. Its beliefs come nearer to an understanding of the world perhaps but the symbols are dead; they are diminished copies of an as yet inaccessible power — that of China (*Où*, p. 29). Korea lacks the integrity Butor demands of a place of influence; it is a stepping stone.

The ruins of Angkor Wat provoke the author's next development: there he ignores the little flute player and thus sheds the black alter ego which has dogged him throughout his work. The element of Angkor is water; we immediately see the symbol of cleansing in Butor's wading through the palace in the midst of the deluge. It cannot be an end in itself, however, as vision is severely restricted within its walls.

The whole book has an atmosphere of ritual increased by the repetitions of image, event and language. Short phrases juxtaposed form near poems within the body of the text and the use of colour and climate reinforce the feeling. The constant taking up again of certain incidents, each time with a little more information given, includes the reader in the development which is taking place throughout the book.

In Korea and Angkor the past was important but it has no connection with the present, hence these are incomplete environments and must be rejected. Only when this has been done can come Santa Barbara and its trial by fire. After such a symbolic death and rebirth

61

the author and his wife (whom we find here for the first time accompanying him in his development) are ready for the final initiation. Before it happens, however, Butor passes through another inter-element: snow. He is attracted by the religion of the Mormons — perhaps only intellectually as he is travelling with colleagues from the university. Obviously he is digressing from his real path because he sees nothing on his way to Brigham Young University; snow blinds him, the car he is in skids constantly and only when he leaves does the magnificent scenery of the Rockies appear. Interesting as are the origins of the Church of the Latter Day Saints, their present-day teaching proves to be full of restrictions and petty prohibitions. Their basis was false — perhaps because it came directly from the eastern seaboard of America and hence directly from Europe without being tempered by the studies of the distant past and of the importance of group over individual that are implied by a passage through the Orient. The Mormons developed in the wrong direction, the true one is practised by the Indians in their dances and rituals. Theirs is a belief which has the purity, clarity and flexibility of the air itself, one which encompasses the whole environment and integrates itself into this greater whole. The ultimate site is the universe and the Indians have it within their grasp, unlimited, timeless.

With Butor, his reader has travelled all round the physical world they live in; if he is aware of what he has read, he will also realize that he has followed a path of development which has gradually shown him the way to a much fuller understanding of his situation in the environment. Butor's pilgrimage has led from the shared personal space of an apartment to a town, a continent and the rest of the world. It has delved into the distant past and, if we include Fourier's universe as a true site, into a hypothetical future. This does not mean, however, that we should all become globe-trotters like Butor himself. Always, as in the Indian dances, as the Venetian can identify with St. Mark's, the outer world is a reflection of the inner self; Vernier's Columbus and the Columbus of *L'oeil des Sargasses*[14] are but two sides of the same explorer.

We find the intimate connection between a person and his world shown in *Les Sept Femmes de Gilbert le Mauvais*, Butor's study of Proust. Marcel identifies with his room, to each of his rooms is attached a person and each person brings a whole outside world. The room in Combray is inextricably entwined with his mother and his childhood, the first room in Paris incorporates Odette and through her the Verdurin's society and so on. The inter-relationship of people and environment is irrefutable. Also, as we have seen in many of the books examined, literary texts are woven into the history of any place; one man's experience expressed in words is accessible as a help to the succeeding generations. This too Proust illustrates, for each room has its text: Combray, *François le Champi*; Tansonville, the work of the Goncourts; works of art criticism (Ruskin) find themselves side by side with memories (Chateaubriand, Saint-Simon), and easily acceptible, imagined reality (Balzac) with the more distant kind (*The Thousand and One Nights*). All levels we have already seen in the sites discussed are encapsulated here. Butor's world must perforce incorporate every aspect from mystery through myth to fact and object. He explores it bit by bit for himself, translates his findings and his methods into his work and offers it to his reader as a guide in his own personal journeying.

The world provides its own key in the centres it has created. All are joined like knots in a vast network of significance, each one connected to a variety of threads; the image brings us back to Bleston where Anne is Ariadne to Revel's Theseus. She sells him the map by which he can come to understand the labyrinth. His diary is our first guide, his name the key to his function. Butor created them all as an inaugural lesson on how to read a site; he built an imaginary town and interpreted it. Everyone of his books since *L'Emploi du Temps*, has provided a similar map and guide to some combination of place, culture and people — usually existant and within the possible experience of Butor's readers — by its combination of form, lay-out and approach to the material on hand. By his very oscillation between real and imaginary sites, the author maintains the dialectic essential to writing while providing a lens through which we see our surroundings anew with a clarity which increases our appreciation of their complexity and richness.[15]

CHAPTER III: FOOTNOTES

1 Bleston contains many elements drawn from Manchester and Liverpool; see Appendix II and also J. Walters, *The Novels of Michel Butor* (University of London, Ph.D. thesis, 1968) and J. B. Howitt, "Michel Butor and Manchester," *Nottingham French Studies*, XII, 2 (October 1973) pp. 74-85.

2 *L'Emploi du Temps*, p. 10: "That air to which I was henceforth condemned for a whole year ... I had felt quite clearly that it contained sly vapours ... which succeeded in plunging me into the terrible apathy from which I have just awakened."

[3] *L'Emploi du Temps*, pp. 146-148, 161, 171, 174 and p. 27 note 11 of this text.

[4] Léonce Peillard, *Biblio* (June 1963), p. 8.

[5] "Sites," *Répertoire III*, pp. 25-31. This essay was first published as an introduction to J. Richer, *La Géographie Sacrée du Monde Grec* (Paris: Hachette, 1967).

[6] See below Chapter VI: Livres.

[7] See F. C. St. Aubyn: "Michel Butor's America," *Kentucky Foreign Language Quarterly*, II, 1 (1964) and "A propos de *Mobile*: Deuxième entretien avec Michel Butor," *French Review*, XXXVIII, 4 (February 1965).

[8] *Description de San Marco*, p. 13: "Those who speak Venetian, those whose mother tongue is Italian, those who speak it fluently, those learning it, those who can struggle along very well for a few days and those who prefer not to take the risk of leaving their own language."

[9] G. Raillard, *Michel Butor*, "Dialogue avec M. Butor," p. 266.

[10] *Description*, p. 32: "Un jeu de citations est une interprétation, et sans jamais heurter de front l'orthodoxie, la bible de Saint-Marc va nous donner une adaptation venétienne du Catholicisme, souvent fort éloignée de la tradition romaine." (A play of quotations is an interpretation, and without ever opposing the orthodox view directly St. Mark's Bible will give us a Venetian adaptation of Catholicism which is often a long way from the Roman tradition.)

[11] *Description*, pp. 45-46: "Venise, avec son contrôle du commerce barbaresque, avec son ghetto, ses liaisons avec les royaumes de terre ferme, comme point de convergence des groupes dispersés à Babel. Orgueil, audace de Venice, la basilique et son campanile comme lieu où les langues viennent se retrouver, les différents peuples s'entendre, la ville de la Pentecôte." (Venice with its control of Levantine trade, its ghetto, its link with the kingdoms on dry land, as the point where the groups dispersed from Babel converge. The pride, the audacity of Venice, the basilica and its bell tower as the place where languages meet, different peoples come to reach an understanding, the town of Pentecost.)

[12] See also J. Roudaut, "Parenthèse sur la place occupée par l'étude intitulée *6 810 000 litres d'eau par seconde* parmi les autres ouvrages de Michel Butor," *Nouvelle Revue Française*, XXVIII, 165 (September 1966), pp. 498-509.

[13] We are reminded of Gaston Bachelard's study of the elements in his critical work and of the fact that Butor was his student.

[14] Editions Lettera Amorosa (Belgium, 1972).

[15] For the American bicentenary Butor produced *USA 76, Bicentenaire Kit* (Plate 12), consisting of a large box containing a series of prints by Monory, numerous objects and documents and Butor's own commentary on the USA in the form of an extended catalogue of the collection — a new museum.

CHAPTER IV

Musées

In moving from sites to museums we continue to be concerned with historical density, but now in the realm of smaller objects, individual works of art and artefacts rather than that of the social collectivity which makes up a total environment — though of course many sites can be considered museums, museums as sites, and we could justify the inclusion of the description of St. Mark's Basilica or of Rome under this heading almost as well as under the preceding one. We must always remember that every detail in Michel Butor's work is multi-faceted and that the arbitrary divisions drawn in this study in an attempt to deal with the material in a coherent fashion must be discarded, the chapters super-imposed and their contents interwoven before a real appreciation of Butor's work can be gained.

As always Butor puts us on the path to comprehension of his intentions, this time by his use of Bleston Museum. He describes it succinctly: blackened Ionic columns outside, a staircase which branches so that the visitors going in do not take the same path as those coming out, and nine exhibition rooms in chronological order (pp. 69-70). The archeological room contains a few Egyptian scarabs, a Greek vase, Coptic fabric, Roman coins and a number of funerary monuments found in Bleston itself. The second room has seventeenth-century clothes and furniture, the eighth holds nineteenth-century paintings, and the ninth local modern work. The middle five rooms house eighteen eighteenth-century tapestries depicting the life of Theseus. Butor's message appears clearly: the origins of Western Europe are present for all to see in the objects from Ancient Egypt, Greece, Christian Egypt-Arab tradition, and Rome, followed by those from the period of religious strife and schism (we remember the two cathedrals and the story of Cain); then occupying by far the most space and also the central position in the arrangement of the rooms in the building (in the rooms between the important numbers of three and seven)[1] are the tapestries with the hero of which Revel identifies himself and which we, the readers, use in our attempts to understand the situation. We see the giant turtle in Plaisance Gardens, Anne as Ariadne, Rose as Phaedre, Revel in a foreign land. Butor describes carefully the panels which are most important: the childhood of Theseus, his trials before reaching Athens, recognition by his father (George Burton), the slaying of the Minotaur, abandonment of Ariadne, Theseus as King of Athens, his descent into hell and finally his exile. The direction Theseus will then take is unknown and perhaps his alternatives are suggested in the diverse ideologies of the paintings in the next gallery in the museum. These are a Constable, a Turner, some Pre-Raphaelites and local portraits of business men. From these develop the modern art.

A progression from age to age is indicated by the linear arrangment of the galleries. The various levels of present time can be seen in the tapestries, some of which present different times side by side so that the observer must recognize the multiplication of the hero and organize the events sequentially. That a study of the objects should produce a change in the observer is implied by the divided upper part of the staircase while the roots of past and present in the city are united in the single lower flight. We see the exhibits as products of their surroundings — the tapestries like Revel imported from France — and realize how much influence the past has on the present and the future, for the last two rooms of the museum are in some ways Revel's future. Museums then contain the past, render it stable and therefore to a certain extent comprehensible, but still, by the continual addition of new objects, express a dynamic sense of questing for greater understanding.

The concept of a museum as a place of individual enrichment and growth within a social context is thus set up as early as 1957. In the next ten years museums are mentioned from time to time in Butor's writings (*Degrés*; Le musée de l'homme, *Mobile*; the Vermont Quilt Museum) but the idea is not developed by the author himself until 1967 when *Portrait de l'artiste en jeune singe* is situated within the walls of Harburg Castle. Here we are dealing with an existing museum and library and the growth of a person within it.[2] The young Butor studies the objects around him in conjunction with the books available in order to move back through the history of the castle, understand its position in the outside world and his own in relation to the pattern thus formed. Also, if the reader wishes, he may visit the castle for himself and assimilate into his own pro-

1. *Michel Butor* by Gregory Masurovsky.

2. *Michel Butor* collage by Jiri Kolár, used here on the cover of *L'Arc* 39.

3. Jade disk, Chinese prehistoric.

LA GRANGE, chef-lieu de La Fayette, TEXAS.

La mer la nuit.

MARSHALL, pays de l'opportunité.

Il rêvait.

Le lac Ouachita.

MARSHALL, chef-lieu de Harrison.

Dans la première de ses immenses magnifiques planches consacrées aux oiseaux d'Amérique, John James Audubon (1780-1851), l'un des plus grands amoureux de la nature américaine, a représenté le dindon sauvage mâle.

EL DORADO.

EL DORADO, ARKANSAS, État de lourd été.

Il rêvait qu'il était grand.

L'Église catholique romaine, — passé la frontière de l'Ouest,

EL DORADO, OKLAHOMA, — la réserve des Indiens Osages.

Deux coucous à bec jaune, sur un feuillage tacheté, celui de gauche montrant son ventre blanc, celui de droite saisissant le corps d'un grand papillon.

MARSHALL.

GREENWOOD, comté de Sébastien, État de la fleur de pommier.

Elle rêvait qu'elle était belle...

La caverne mystique, — passé le père des fleuves,

GREENWOOD, MISSISSIPI, le profond Sud.

BENTON, avec ses mines de bauxite, chef-lieu de Salines.

Qu'elle remportait un prix de beauté...

La caverne du Grand-Ouragan, — passé le père des fleuves, mais plus au nord,

BENTON, TENNESSEE, le Sud.

La fauvette protonotaire, ses pattes agrippant une liane, tête et ventre jaune éclatant, queue en éventail blanche et noire, — passé la frontière rectiligne du sud,

BENTON, LOUISIANE, le profond Sud.

La fauvette bleue à dos jaune, perchée sur un grand iris saumon, dit le drapeau de Louisiane, — passé la frontière rectiligne du nord,

BENTON.

Deux couples de colombes pleureuses se béquetant sur un buisson à grosses fleurs blanches.

MARSHALL, chef-lieu de Salines, MISSOURI, middle-west.

Le ciel nocturne qui pâlit.

LA GRANGE, chef-lieu de Lewis.

L'étoile du matin.

CORNING. — En continuant vers le nord,

CORNING, IOWA, — la réserve des Indiens Tamas. — A l'équinoxe de printemps, quand le jour se lève à

CORNING,

4. *Mobile* pp. 12-13 showing Butor's use of typography to express geographical relationships.

— Tu as vu? — L'eau. — Ciel d'avril. — Vous voyez... — Robe verte. — Formi-

Autour douze apôtres baptisant chacun une nation — Jacques le Majeur remplacé par Marc — caressant la tête d'un caté-chumène nu, enfoncé jusqu'à la ceinture dans une cuve de marbre, un puits, une citerne, sous les murs d'une ville, à l'étonnement d'un indigène en costume local.

SANCTUS MATHEUS
baptise en Ethiopie
SANCTUS SIMON
baptise en Egypte
SANCTUS THOMAS
baptise en Inde
SANCTUS ANDREA
baptise en Carie
SANCTUS PETRUS
baptise à Rome
SANCTUS BARTOLOMEUS
baptise en Inde
SANCTUS TADEUS
baptise en Mésopotamie
SANCTUS MATIAS
baptise en Palestine
SANCTUS MARCUS
baptise à Alexandrie
SANCTUS JOHANNES
baptise à Jérusalem
SANCTUS JACOBUS MINOR
baptise en Judée
SANCTUS PHILIPPUS
baptise en Phrygie

Sans qu'on puisse discerner ici d'orientation géographique.
Modèle byzantin sans doute, dont on a remplacé certains détails.

dable! — Chevelure acajou. — Soleil de mai. — Lèvres gitane. — Ongles pink

Sur les pendentifs, les quatre Pères de l'Eglise grecque :

SANCTUS JOHANNES CHRYSOSTOMUS
SANCTUS GREGORIUS NAZIANZENUS
SANCTUS BASILIUS EPISCOPUS
SANCTUS ATHANASIUS

Leurs chasubles ornées de croix noires sur fond blanc.
La porte qui donne dans l'église. Deux des piliers, deux des colonnes de porphyre en enfilade, les bénitiers, la lumière pleu-vant de la grande baie.
Le va-et-vient des Ethiopiens, des Ethiopiennes, des Egyptiens, des Egyptiennes, des Hindous et Hindoues...

dawn. — Fatiguée? — Meravigliosa! — Vous croyez... — Un pigeon. — L'eau. — Tu es belle. — Bella donna. — La lumière. — L'or. — Really? — Ciel de février.

Sur le mur, au-dessus de la porte, le Festin d'Hérode.

PUELLAE SALTANTI IMPAVIT MATER
« Or comme Hérode célébrait son anniversaire de naissance, la fille d'Hérodiade dansa en public et plut tant à Hérode qu'il s'engagea par serment à lui accorder tout ce qu'elle demanderait. Endoc-trinée par sa mère, elle lui dit : « Donne-moi ici, sur un plat, la tête de Jean le Baptiste. » Salomé, robe rubis tissée d'or, longs pendentifs d'hermine aux coudes, bordure d'hermine à la fente de la robe jusqu'à la naissance de la fesse, danse en tenant au-dessus de la chevelure d'or le plat d'or où repose la longue tête à longue barbe de saint Jean.

Par la haute fenêtre en face, le ciel, les nuages.

— Vous plaît? — Rosetta. — Robe violette. — Vous vous connaissiez? — Je viens d'Alexandrie. — L'eau. — Vu? — It's fantastic! — Robe jaune. — Magnificent! — Vous suivez la... — L'ombre. — On peut? — Magnif... — Wond... — Soleil

5. *Description de San Marco*, pp. 96-97, typography used to illustrate the architectural form of St. Mark's Basilica, Venice.

6.-7. *Illustrations* pp. 140-41 and *Litanie d'eau* p. 26. Below: Butor's text in its original form accompanied by Masurovsky's engraving. Top right; the same text reset to achieve the same effect without a visual image.

Menace sur la mer de chaud nickel   croule animal violet
sous les drapeaux du ciel de fonte gronde   buisson fantôme
violet s'étire   sombre   se dresse   se relâche dans son halo noir
à l'horizon   va léger   museau violet   sur l'eau de bronze vif
explose
animal violet   qui dort sous le ciel   brun   qui file sur la mer
qui roule   turquoises   émeraudes jais   améthystes et escarboucles
tremble doux   creux noir   s'aplanit   penche tendre méduse   violette
à l'horizon de fonte   rêve de lune   brune   remue d'eau brune
sous le ciel   qui mousse   aérien   trébuche   vient multiple cercle

De froid lichen   noir qui tombe   sur la mer violette
titube   hésite   souple ombre brune   sur l'horizon de bronze   croule
chevelure salée   buisson jaune   se plisse   chaude
sous le ciel   qui respire l'eau s'effondre   léger   lait bière café
sang vif   se raidit   se balance   sombre   s'arque sur la mer
à l'horizon   douce   lymphe   sueur   encre   tendres larmes
revient   dans le ciel qui l'engloutit   flageole   s'agite dans l'eau
aicool   lave   goudron   bitume   se hérisse   se calme s'adoucit
se cambre sur l'horizon   sous le ciel de fonte se reprend
mer de soupirs file   se cabre   s'étend   soupirs de l'eau

faucons canards,
verdiers têtes bleues,
faucons épaules rouges,

qui sort, par la rivière Niagara qui sort
du lac, du lac Érié et se jette, Niagara,
Érié, et se jette dans l'Ontario à environ
neuf milles de ce dernier lac...

compose

Menace sur la mer de chaud nickel croule animal violet
sous les drapeaux du ciel de fonte gronde buisson fantôme
violet s'étire sombre se dresse se relâche dans son halo noir
à l'horizon va léger museau violet sur l'eau de bronze vif
explose
animal violet qui dort sous le ciel brun qui file sur la mer
qui roule turquoises émeraudes jais améthystes et escarboucles
tremble doux creux noir s'aplanit penche tendre méduse violette
à l'horizon de fonte rêve de lune brune remue d'eau brune
sous le ciel qui mousse aérien trébuche vient multiple cercle

140

De froid lichen noir qui tombe sur la mer violette
titube hésite souple ombre brune sur l'horizon de bronze croule
chevelure salée buisson jaune se plisse chaude
sous le ciel qui respire l'eau s'effondre léger lait bière café
sang vif se raidit se balance sombre s'arque sur la mer
à l'horizon douce lymphe sueur encre tendres larmes
revient dans le ciel qui l'engloutit flageole s'agite dans l'eau
alcool lave goudron bitume se hérisse se calme s'adoucit
se cambre sur l'horizon sous le ciel de fonte se reprend
mer de soupirs file se cabre s'étend soupirs de l'eau

141

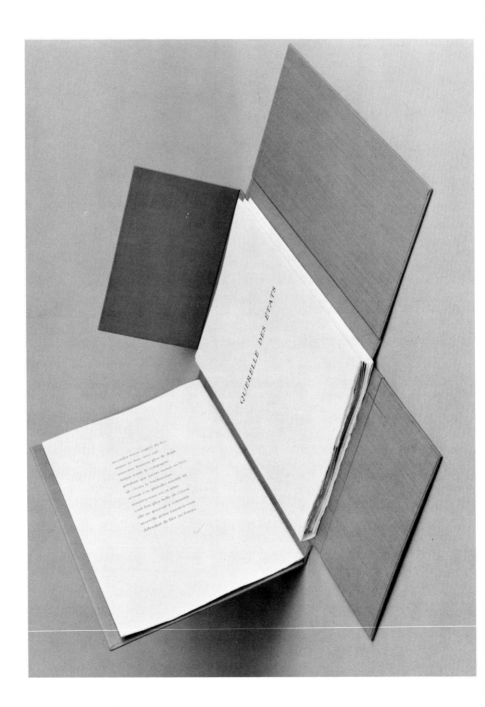

8.-9. *Querelle des États* (Butor and Bryen), displayed above. Below: last triptych. "États" (states) is the term used for the different colour blocks of a print. Here are stages superimposed to create the central image. Butor's text is layered in a similar way.

10. *Tourmente* No. 11 (Butor and Hérold), is one of a series of poems and posters that Butor made with various artist friends as a response to the political upheavals in France in 1968.

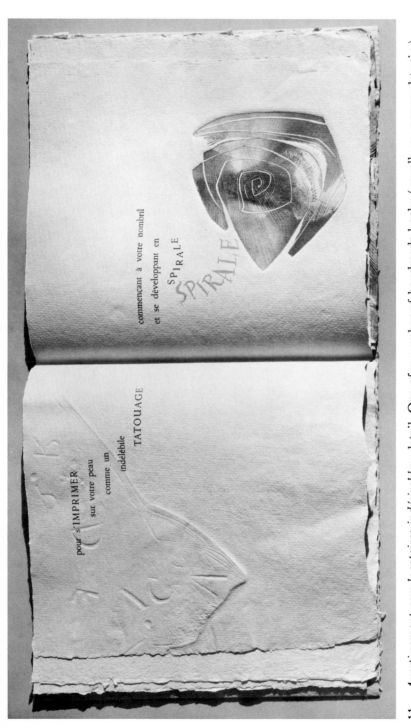

pour s'IMPRIMER
sur votre peau
comme un
indélébile
TATOUAGE

commençant à votre nombril
et se développant en
SPIRALE
SPIRALE

11. *Avertissement aux locataires indésirables*, detail. One of a number of handmade books (usually on personal topics) that Staritsky and Butor have created together.

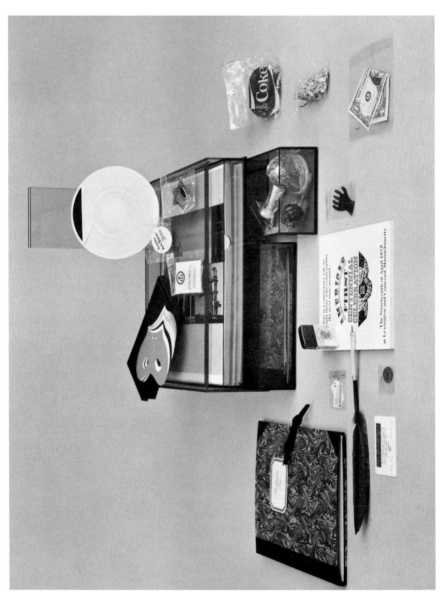

12. *Bicentenaire kit* object assembled by Butor and Monory as a commentary
the bicentenary of USA

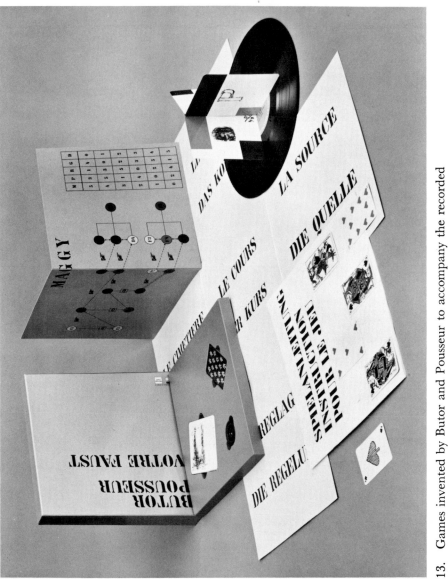

13. Games invented by Butor and Pousseur to accompany the recorded version of their opera *Votre Faust*.

14.-15.   Letters from Michel Butor; for the most part original collages using postcards.

St Laurent du Var, le 26 mars 1971

Chère Jennifer,

nous avons enfin déménagé, non pour la maison que nous tentions sur le
collier. — Cependant nous avons dû renoncer à cause de différentes égales, par
pour un double appartement au Croisette — Jennie trop, d'un immeuble en
cours d'achèvement dans un faubourg. Nous avons les deux d'un côté; le me le
l'autre; mais nous n'avons encore ni le chauffage central (est-il à feu? ni pas)
ce mois-ci —) ni l'ascenseur, ni le Téléphone. Tout cela n'écho pas à peu, à
Crois- Tout fonctionne parfaitement nous demandions encore ...

le portrait de l'Artiste? à un pas encore traduit en anglais.

Ki - le nos grands problème ou l'accompagnement de filles au l'école. Avan nous
menos les deltanes ni nous pouvons loges une jeune fille qui viendrait ...

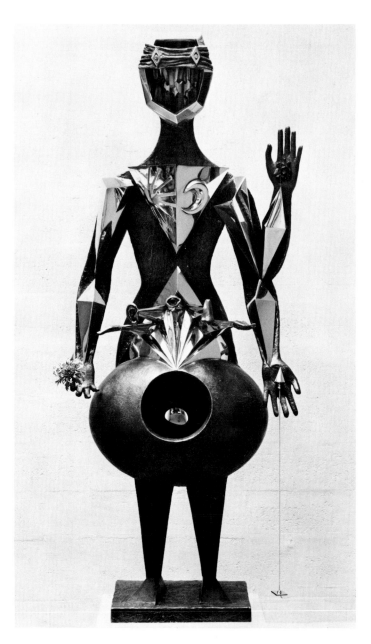

16.   *Le Grand Transparent*, by Jacques Hérold. Sculpture which is the subject of Butor's *Petites liturgies intimes pour hâter l'avenement du Grand Transparent* (1972) and which was made at the request of André Breton for the International Surrealism Exhibition, Paris 1947.

gress objects which Butor has not chosen to use. The possibilities are open and endless, especially as the reader must put together for himself the fragments and allusions given by the author. No two readers will come to identical conclusions concerning *Portrait de l'artiste en jeune singe.*

In this chapter we are concerned primarily with the castle itself and the objects it contains, but a sketch of the structure of *Portrait* and the role of the books within it is essential for a full appreciation of the role of the objects described. The book depends on the constant inter-relation of reality and fantasy and these are juxtaposed in alternate chapters dealing in turn with daytime happenings and the dreams which follow during the night. The dreams are conscious symbolic creations whereas the events and environment are drawn from Butor's memory of a summer spent in Germany in his youth. The title of the book has reference to the alchemists' use of the image of a monkey to illustrate their position as the apes of God in their attempts to understand the universe and recreate it in the laboratory, and all the chapters concerning dreams have titles tracing the seven stages of the alchemical process.

The dreams retrace young Butor's development by transforming him into the prince of the Second Calender's Tale in *The Thousand and One Nights.* (This young man is turned into a monkey and saves himself from death by his ability to write.) The text is a very important one for the full understanding of Butor's capriccio, hence its position at the highest points of the libraries of both Harburg and Weissenstein.

All the works quoted point the way to the past, to alchemy and above all to the Middle Ages when western man first took an interest in his own history, the Orient (Charlemagne was in contact with Haroun-al-Rashid), and science, and the time he began to express himself copiously in writing. The books mentioned reflect the two main themes of dream and travel. The future can only be improved by a knowledge of the past; Thomas Mann's *Joseph in Egypt* is offered as an example. Joseph, like any alchemist and like Butor himself, is exiled and finds a second home in Egypt. His wisdom manifests itself in the interpretation of dreams. Here is a third level of allegory which reinforces both the alchemical imagery and Butor's main theme. It may be assumed that all of Butor's readers will be familiar with the biblical story and so the title of Mann's novel offers an accessible key to the different levels.

Egypt is at the root of all mystery and all wisdom. The very title

67

of Kircher's *Oedipus Aegyptiacus* shows that there has been a question posed whose hidden answer may be found in Ancient Egypt. Kircher's other works are cited as examples of the importance of physical and spiritual exploration: *America Illustrata, China Illustrata, Iter Extaticum* (the way of ecstacy). For Butor Father Athanasius Kircher is Uriel, the archangel, who plays an important role in eastern liturgy and whose name means "Light of God". Kircher was a contemporary of Jacob Boehme and both sought a cosmic solution through study of the Bible. Boehme's *Mysterium Magnum* combines the alchemical world with religious dogma. It is important to *Portrait* because of its study of the seven days of Creation in which religious, mythological, astrological and alchemical elements are used in the presentation and analysis. These authors wrote in Old German and Latin, proof that Butor found them more difficult than certain others who studied similar problems. The clarity of Basile Valentin's work *Les Douze Clés de la Philosophie* is indicated by the fact that it is quoted in French, as is the work of Nicolas Flamel. (French, being a modern language, is used as a sign of accessibility.)

Alchemy itself, besides defining the symbolic aim of *Portrait*, encompasses the idea that every book is a hermetic one. Every book helps its reader to an understanding of the universe if he only realizes how it must be read. Truth must always be sought beneath the surface of appearance just as the meaning of a dream may be explained. The choice of the double structure of *Portrait* and the use of other authors offer flexibility and multiple possibilities for exploration. By means of books the reader is trying to grasp an ever changing world. Ovid's *Metamorphoses* supports the theory and so does *Les Papillons de Surinam*, an eighteenth-century treatise by Maria Sibylla Merinan, which bears the Latin subtitle "Dissertio de generatione et metamorphosibus insectorum surinamensium" (dissertation on *birth* and *metamorphosis*).

To understand anything properly man needs to dream, to be a visionary, and, in order to stress the importance of the books of fantasy he has chosen, Butor adds *L'art de se rendre heureux par les rêves* and *Les rêves et les moyens de les diriger*. Their titles make their purpose clear. Modern works (Kubin: *The Other Side*, Werfel: *The stars of the unborn*) project the idea of dream into the geographical and chronological distance, while the *Cabinet des fées* brings it back to France in the eighteenth century, the time when *The Thousand and One Nights* had just been translated.

The movement of *Portrait* goes from France, the knowledge Butor gained there and carried with him (Fulcanelli: *Les Demeures Philosophales*), to Mediaeval Germany, to the world of Harburg which has to be understood, and then out to Egypt, country of rebirth. The objects to be found in the castle follow the direction given by the books, reinforcing and giving material form to their teaching. As we have seen in the very structure of *Portrait* which is built on the alchemically powerful numbers of seven and three — three sections, seven days of creation, seven weeks of stay, seven words in the title — the whole pattern is supported by the metaphor of an alchemical experiment, with the castle itself as athanor. There are seven stages that are a long slow initiation shown in three levels simultaneously: physical experiment in the laboratory, study and writing of allegorically disguised texts concerning the philosopher's stone and the spiritual development of the person concerned. We recognize the parallels between the museum and its mineral collection and Butor's interest in the physical world, the young man's reading and the text of *Portrait* itself and the growth Butor is tracing together with the one he hopes to provoke in his reader. During the seven weeks of his stay in H, Butor learns seven patience games and dreams seven dreams.

The patience games, taught to him by the Count, are games containing their own solution. The player must accept the rules and go on with the experiment until he succeeds. Thus he may go through a vast number of repetitions and permutations before reaching his aim. The seven games mentioned are each wider in context than the last beginning with the *Almanach de Gotha* and the *Moyens de parvenir* both showing ways of joining an elite, and ending with the *Roue des planètes* when the initiation period is drawing to a close.

The castle itself is hermetic in form. Begun in the Middle Ages when the power of alchemy was at its height, it has a strong outer wall enclosing a small village and seven towers of varying shapes around an inner courtyard where only the Count and Butor live. There is even a witch's house at the gate. The edifice stands high on a cliff above the town, showing its superiority in its very position. The main hall, the Knights' room, has paintings of alchemical allegories on the ceiling: Mercury, Medea, and Perseus rescuing Andromeda from the monster. Maier's book *Museum Hermeticum* indicates the importance of the knowledge Harburg holds and also the effort that must be made to understand it.

In any development of this kind progress is only made through death and rebirth, hence one of the greatest treasures in the museum is an ivory crucifix whose Christ has a changing expression, sometimes sad, sometimes smiling. There are also a tapestry and an old manuscript[3] of the life of Joseph which support both the above theme and that of the books discussed above, but which are not themselves mentioned by Butor.

Constant juxtaposition is made between a contemplative life and a worldly one. In sculpture there are the calm figures of Tilman Riemenschneider and the coquettish saints of Veit Stoss. A similar contrast is to be seen in the fine altar-piece painted by Bernard Strigel, for when open it displays scenes of the life of St. Anne and while closed it shows portraits of a worldly pair, Simon de Montfort and his wife the Princess von Oettingen.

To show the levels on which wisdom should be sought, Butor selects three series of engravings which depict personal folly, social irresponsibility leading to experience and divine revelation, and which simultaneously suggest a movement towards the past to seek the lost understanding. The engravings are William Hogarth's *Rake's Progress* (English 18th century), Jacques Callot's *Les Misères et Malheurs de la Guerre* (French 17th century) and Albrect Dürer's *Apocalypse* (German late 15th century). Taken within the alchemical image they show (as the chosen books do) a degeneration from true spiritual searching to the desire to make gold for personal satisfaction. (One of Hogarth's prints includes an alchemist and his athanor.)

The point is made again in Butor's citation of the portrait of Charlemagne in robes as priest-king of his people — the symbol of unity between the spiritual and secular, soul and body. The image recalls the structure of *Portrait* where conscious thought and dream are joined to achieve a result beyond the reach of either. That the way to such understanding is long is shown by the presence of Dürer's *Melancholia*.[4] She sits despondently among the tools and symbols of hermetic knowledge which she does not appear to be able to use. Like the young Butor and like the reader of *Portrait* she must understand the significance of the objects around her before they can be of use.

The young Butor works back into the history of the castle by means of a guidebook, *Die Harburg im Ries*,[5] which stresses above all by quotation from the records of the castle executioner the important role of death in any progress. Here the crucifix and the *Apocalypse* come to mind and we realize that the engravings reflect not only the general conditions and attitudes of their time but also reflect directly on the history of the castle: plague, famine, war, and libertinage are all intertwined in the growth of Harburg together with the religion, alchemy, theosophy and fantasy used in turn to try and understand it. Butor was given the keys to Harburg and allowed to discover its treasures as he might, so that he had to find a method for his own study. In this, his visit to Weissenstein Castle at Pommersfelden is of great assistance; the plan and decoration of the castle describe the young Butor's aims quite clearly. Any reader who may visit the castle will find startling confirmation of the movement described in *Portrait*.

Weissenstein Castle was built in the eighteenth century by Lothar Franz von Shoenborn, Elector and Supreme Knight of the Holy Roman Empire, Prince-Archbishop of Bamberg and Mayence. An imposing baroque building, it has an unusual tutelary god for the palace of an archbishop: Hermes. He stands on the roof overlooking the central courtyard and is also the central figure of the fresco which covers the ceiling of the vast entrance hall, dominating the main staircase in such a way that it appears to lead directly to the god and the four continents that surround him with their riches. It would seem that the path to Hermes — that of the alchemists — is the way to complete understanding, for the castle beneath him contains paintings of gods, mortals, animals, flowers and fruit of every kind imaginable. The god himself is in the pose normally reserved for the ascending Christ, a point we remember ironically when we think of the scenes from Tasso's *Jerusalem Delivered* which decorate one of the galleries. The top floor of the foyer is decorated with Jupiter's love affairs establishing the position both of the gods and of metamorphosis, alchemical transformation leading to supremacy. The floor below bears the labours of Hercules — reference to the same thing but this time within the power of a demi-god. In alcoves near the stairs are stucco statues, again referring to hermetic experiment: Jupiter, Urania holding an open book and pointing to a globe, Juno and her peacock whose feathers show the colours of transmutation and a goddess holding a laurel wreath for the victor.

The visitor to Pommersfelden is not allowed to go up the staircase immediately, however (for tourists also follow the route described by Butor in *Portrait*); first he must descend into the Garden Room, which Butor calls the grotto because of its strange appearance. Built from natural rocks and shells the room seems to be a real cave and contains statues of the four seasons and the four elements. The significance of the mineral collection at Harburg is obvious seen in its rightful position as the foundation of the edifice.

Weissenstein is a monument to Butor's ambition as it stretches beyond the reach of Harburg, out of the Holy Roman Empire he has come to understand and beyond into new mysteries, new learning hinted at by the books he has read. He must go out and use what he has learned. He chooses to seek Hermes Trismagisthus at his source, thus proving the castles/museums to be sources of historical vitality and not dead worlds closed upon themselves.

Museums do not deal exclusively with the past, however. They attract new objects constantly and their function is to establish a relationship between the collection and the visitors who come to look at it. This is usually done by means of a guide-book on sale at the entrance to the building and labels describing each exhibit's geographical and historical origins. We have seen that the literary references and quotations in *Portrait* are inseparable from the castle and its contents, that architecture, artefact and text are mutually explanatory, each forming a setting for the other in the mind of the observer. But we have also dealt in reality with words alone, unless we have made the effort, unusual in a reader of a piece of fiction, to visit the castles or seek out copies of the works of art described.

Butor has dealt with a similar situation already; in 1964 he published a book in the collection "Le Musée de Poche" on the work of the artist Jacques Hérold. The book begins and ends with a dialogue between Butor and Hérold and this surrounds the critical text written by Butor. The whole volume is interspersed with illustrations of Hérold's work. This presentation results in the feeling for the reader that he is asking questions of the paintings themselves, receiving answers and musing on the information given until it produces new questions. Butor learns of Hérold's past and the artist's desire to express what is below the surface of the objects around him, and we the readers are confirmed in our desire to understand the works of art around us which, as the expression of the artist's search for understanding, can help us in ours.

The sources of Butor's own development were drawn from a real museum-library in which he recognized the significant elements. A year after the publication of *Portrait* the author published a museum of his own exhibits selected and arranged as he wished in *Répertoire III*. The organization of the volume shows much the same preoccupations as those which shape *L'Arc* No. 39 in the same year. *Répertoire III* opens and closes with a piece of theoretical criticism (Arts et Métiers), the second and third pieces are concerned with the historical and geographical power of a site, the two before the last with an art exhibition and opera (Spectacles), while the main body of the work consists of a number of essays on literature and art. Again text and plastic art are presented as two facets of the expression of similar experience. The essays are in chronological order from Hans Holbein to Mark Rothko and present a certain picture of the civilization of Western Europe. If we consider here the essays on painters we shall see that Butor has in fact recreated the quest that went backwards into the centre of Harburg and beyond, but this time it moves forward into New York and on.

Let us take the essays and artists one by one and follow Butor's path. "Un tableau vu en détail," an analysis of Hans Holbein the younger's painting *Francis I's ambassadors at the court of Henry VIII*, teaches how to read a painting by examining it detail by detail, object by object. It also presents a total world view at a time when the universe was believed to be stable, Ptolemaic astronomy ruled the heavens, the great chain of being established order amongst all things and symbolic representation was understood by all. Jean de Dinteville and Georges de Selve are in a world they know, but Holbein inserts an element of doubt in his placing of the skull in the foreground. The artist is exploring a different world from that of the politicians.

In "La Corbeille de l'Ambrosienne" Butor writes about a still life by Caravaggio. His mode of discussion places the work among other renderings of the same subject by the artist and also sums up the changing attitude of critics towards the painting, the way it has been understood through the centuries. Caravaggio has removed all sense of context within his work (though the reader is given a wider one than he had before) and is concerned purely with the object as it defines itself by the forms and colours of its own reality.

The next artist Butor considers is Hokusaï as he works in his series *Thirty-six and ten views of Mount Fuji*. All Hokusaï's prints represent the sacred mountain in an aspect different from the others. He juxtaposes the form of the volcano to other basic shapes in turn, learning from the patterns formed. Not only is he concerned with geographical situation (thus joining Butor on another plane in their celebration of a site) but above all with the multiplicity of appearances. This is taken up again in the following essay, "Claude Monet ou le Monde Renversé," where we see the very form of objects disappear behind the shifting surface of light and colour.

73

The outside world has vanished in its apparent reality and we are obliged to modify our modes of perception. Picasso distorts the presentation of the world even further in his efforts to make its meaning clear ("La suite dans les images"). In his work significance is born not so much with reference to an outside measure as within the body of the painting itself. The surface of objects has been torn away, as in Hérold's work, the better to reveal their significance and this is cumulative within the life and work of the artist. Mondrian goes further still ("Le carré et son habitant"), reducing the world to its basic lines, visible and invisible. He writes in *Natural Reality, Abstract Reality* that his horizontal line represents the horizon and the vertical joins the moon to the earth, hence defining the sky. His squares are suggestions for rooms which will provide harmony. A person looking at a Mondrian painting must scrutinize it, for the slightest deviation of angle or line has immense importance in the austerity of the whole. The work proposes a future which the onlooker must interpret for himself, but is still the presentation of a world view. Mark Rothko seems to leap from presentation to aspiration in his work ("Les Mosquées de New York"). For Butor he provides an oasis of calm in the centre of the modern world of overwhelming objects. He creates the light within which new creation must be made.

Each assumption in painting has been questioned and stripped away as the artist has delved into the nature of the reality of all things. The whole process that Butor has traced through the artists he has chosen reminds us of Hokusaï's plan for himself. In his preface to *A hundred views of Mount Fuji* when he was seventy-four years old he wrote:

From the time I was six years old I have always drawn the form of objects. By fifty I had published a multitude of drawings but nothing I produced before the age of seventy is worth consideration. It was at the age of seventy-three that I understood more or less the structure of the true nature of animals, plants, trees, birds, fish and insects. Thus by eighty I should have made more progress, at ninety I shall penetrate the mystery of objects; by a hundred I shall certainly have reached a marvellous stage and when I am one hundred and ten everything I create, a dot, a line, will be alive. (*Répertoire III*, p. 160)

The quest for understanding and its expression is pursued by artists at all times and each one's experience helps the next to go further. There is no question of improving upon the work of the previous generations, but of filling the gaps in their network of knowledge, of

74

pushing out into the unexplored or the unexpressed. (And this was Vernier's stated aim at the beginning of *Degrés*!)

Museums are therefore collaborative structures of a certain type where the experience of the past is selected, accumulated deliberately and arranged in a manner as clear and overtly didactic as possible. Sites also represent cumulative knowledge born of the inevitable part many generations play in their continual modification, but because they are usually haphazard in their growth they are often less easily comprehensible. Butor believes that individual works of art are also the fruit of collaboration, conscious or unconscious, between the creator in question and his surrounding culture, hence it is not surprising that he has frequently worked together with artists to create books which are the mutual expression of a shared experience.

These works — *Cycle* with Calder (1962), *Rencontre* with Zañartu (1962), (*Mon cher Marc-Jean* (1965) with Marc-Jean Masurovsky), *Litanie d'eau* (1964), *Comme Shirley* (1966), *Western Duo* (1969) with G. Masurovsky, *Dialogue des Règnes* (1967) with J. Hérold, *Michel Butor Tourmente* (1968) with P. Alechinsky, B. Dufour and J. Hérold (Plate 10), *Hoirie Voirie* (1970), *Le Rêve de l'Ammonite* (1974) with Pierre Alechinsky, *Quatre Lettres écrites du Nouveau Mexique* (1971) and *La Querelle des Etats* (1973) with Camille Bryen (Plates 8 and 9), *Une Chanson pour Don Juan* (1972) and *Avertissement aux locataires indésirables* (1974) with Ania Staritsky (Plate 11), and others — are all published in limited editions and hence not easily available,[6] but Butor uses his part of the original process to produce another kind of collaboration, this time with his reader, by republishing his texts together with some other writings, responses to exhibitions he has seen, music he has heard in the two volumes of *Illustrations* published in 1964 and 1969 respectively. These responses are now read by people who have no access to the art works which provided the author's stimulus. Each reader is thus obliged to imagine them for himself and in this way continue the chain of results born of the original experience of the now distant artist. Butor described the process on the cover of *Illustrations II*:

ILLUSTRATIONS
d'images absentes
de textes absents
qui étaient elles-mêmes
qui étaient eux-mêmes

75

DES ILLUSTRATIONS
de textes absents
d'images absentes
qui seraient eux-mêmes
qui seraient elles-mêmes
LEURS ILLUSTRATIONS⁷   (*Ed. G.*)

For as we have seen, words and images, texts and objects are inseparable in Butor's world. He accepts that they should be born one of the other sequentially as in some parts of *Illustrations* or in the *Petites Liturgies Intimes pour hâter l'avènement du Grand Transparent de Jacques Hérold* (a text written for the exhibition of the sculpture (Plate 16) and created in almost the same material, for both Hérold and Butor show Surrealist influence), but prefers that they should emerge simultaneously, either within one creation or from close collaboration between artists, as have some of his other works.

In *Les Mots dans la Peinture* Butor considers the role of words within a painting and around it as extensions of its meaning, adding precision to it. These words give indication by their position and form of some important features of the work itself. Above all Butor considers the words as part of a dialogue within the context of the work. In his own writing quotation of titles, names or passages of text serve a similar purpose, differentiation of typeface attracts the attention of the reader, the content of the quotation then supplies him with necessary information, creating new possibilities by juxtaposition within the book or extension beyond it.

Let us consider in this light the use of quotation within *Portrait de l'artiste en jeune singe*. There are three kinds of quotation. Those in the "Prélude" are taken from alchemical treatises written in French and introduce the reader to the theory of transmutation and the techniques of allegorical and hermetic presentation; they are informative. Then quotation is used in the dream chapters to recall and modify snatches of the past so that they take on a new significance; the Second Calender's Tale is followed closely and rendered more fantastic by the addition of colours and minerals. Finally in the German chapters information and evocative power are combined. On a superficial level the quotations illustrate the daily reading done by the young Butor and provide source material for the dreams, but they evoke a world that is bigger than usual. The mystery of Creation can be glimpsed behind the days of an ordinary week; planets and pagan gods are grouped around the Christian

76

Deity. Aspiration and purity go side by side with crime and the death penalty. And through everything comes an awareness of unceasingly passing time.

Butor creates an awareness of how little time man has at his disposal to read and learn. At the beginning of his journey to the Holy Roman Empire he explores his surroundings and then starts to read. He quotes titles at first without knowing what the works contain, but as his stay draws to an end he quotes more and more. The pace of *Portrait* quickens and references to the executions described in the history of Castle H recur as constant reminders of death. The accelerated rhythm implies frenzied work before departure and the fear of deprivation that departure entails. Simultaneously the quotations signify the workings of a mind which is beginning to realize the many ways in which its knowledge can be combined. We see that the author has the intention of jolting the reader out of his usual reading habits just as Cubist and Surrealist painters incorporated words to produce shock effects of association on their canvases.

Quotations may have great power within a piece of writing, words may transform a canvas, but still the most influential collection of words attached to any work of art or literature is its title. This influences our attitude to the work, being ever-present in our minds and attaching the word firmly to the body of the work. Butor discusses the titles of his own work with G. Charbonnier[8] and those of works of art in *Les Mots dans la Peinture*. His titles evolve as his work progresses, beginning with play on words in *Passage de Milan* — the name of the street and city and also the passing of the bird — and *L'Emploi du Temps* — timetable and the way time is occupied. He continues to a series implying change and constant movement in *La Modification, Degrés, Mobile* and *6 810 000 litres d'eau par seconde*. *Votre Faust* implies a shift of responsibility from the author to his audience and hence an enfolding of them into his dilemma. *Description de San Marco* has affinities with *Portrait de l'artiste en jeune singe* in its intention to present a given subject. The latter title is complex, for not only does it refer to literary antecedents (James Joyce, *Portrait of the artist as a young man* and Dylan Thomas, *Portrait of the artist as a young dog*) but by its choice of a monkey as symbol it both questions the role of the artist as a mere imitator and plunges immediately into the main image of the book, that of alchemy. The latter point is reinforced by the fact of it being a seven word title. The number seven forms a link too with *Les*

77

Sept Femmes de Gilbert le Mauvais, a link which is both literary and double in its allusion both to Proust and to Bluebeard.

Like some of the artists he writes about in *Les Mots dans la Peinture*, he includes himself into his work from time to time. In several of the pieces of fiction there is a teacher of more or less his age, in *Mobile* he appears as "un butor américain," in *L'Arc* as "le butor étoilé" and in *6 810 000 litres d'eau par seconde* as a French visiting professor at the University of Buffalo — a post which Michel Butor held for a term in 1962.

In many ways he resembles the artists he studies. Those he assembles, whether in his criticism or in his fiction, are brought together for a single purpose: to show the vital role that a cultural heritage plays in the creativity of those who are sensitive to its power. Museums for Butor are not mausoleums of dead artefacts, but rather dynamic assemblies of past experience on which the present must draw when pushing towards the future. The notebooks Marco Polo wrote describing his journey to China provided practical help to Christopher Columbus as well as inciting him to search for like marvels himself. The explorations of both stood as examples for the schoolboys of *Degrés*.

The past is a constant source of energy which is available to help man understand his present and move on into a richer future. Butor shows that this force collects in "Museums" which when properly laid out and sensitively explored take their place as the dynamic centres of our culture. He accepts the role of guide and creator as he introduces us first to fictitious collections, then when our awareness has been focused, moves us on to the study of real ones. As always, the movement leads out from books to a world we appreciate more fully in the light of Butor's didactic and evocative structures.

CHAPTER IV: FOOTNOTES

1 See below Chapter VII: Symbolic reflections.

2 For further information see J. Walters, "Literary Alchemy; a study of *Portrait de l'artiste en jeune singe*," *Diacritics*, I, 2 (Winter 1971) and J. Waelti-Walters, *Alchimie et littérature* (Paris: Denoël, Dossiers des Lettres Nouvelles, 1975).

3 Dschami, *Joseph and Zuleika*, Persian 15th century.

4 J. van Lennep, *Art et Alchimie* (Brussels: Editions Meddens, 1966), pp. 201-210, gives an excellent analysis of this work.

⁵ By Dr. Anton Diemand, no date.

⁶ A complete bibliography can be found in M. Butor, *Le Rêve du Démenage-ment*, Vol. 7 (Belgium: Lettera Amorosa, 1975).

⁷ "ILLUSTRATIONS/of absent images/of absent texts/which were them-selves/which were themselves/ILLUSTRATIONS/of absent texts/of absent images/which themselves would be/which themselves would be/THEIR ILLUSTRATIONS."

⁸ G. Charbonnier, *Entretiens avec Michel Butor* (Paris: Gallimard, 1968), pp. 11-13.

CHAPTER V

Spectacles

The spectacles Michel Butor offers to his reader, like the sites and museums, fall into two categories: those he finds and those he creates. This time creation begins with the cinema Revel frequents in Bleston, but as it is used rather more within the historical framework of *L'Emploi du Temps* than as true entertainment we shall not concern ourselves with it here.

The first real spectacle is then *Réseau Aérien*,[1] a radio play commissioned by the French radio and performed first on 16th June 1962. In it Butor experiments with quality of sound. Ten couples on ten planes are flying round the world on their way to or from Nouméa, New Caledonia. One route, across the USA, has daylight for most of the journey, the other flies through the night. The play consists of snatches of conversation interspersed with sound: crowd noise at each airport, percussion also at each landing, aircraft sound to indicate a change of plane and hence of conversation. Each recurrence of one of the ten craft is distinguished by a given number of notes of the *Well-Tempered Clavier* played after the crowd or aeroplane noise, one note for the first plane in the play, two for the second and so on. Butor chooses also to distinguish between night and day by the quality of the sound of the transmission: clavichord in the daytime and piano at night and also a different quality of voice recording to indicate the different time/route: sharper in the day, more muffled at night. The interest of the work lies in the combination of word, tone and modification of relationship between the couples. The interplay of journeys resembles that described in *La Modification*, so it is interesting to see that Butor writes about the play:

L'unité d'identification n'est plus l'acteur mais le couple, mais c'est le même acteur que l'on entend dans le premier couple des deux avions qui vont à Nouméa, il constitue un personnage double qui s'écartèle autour du monde pour se recomposer à la fin.[2]

The idea is similar to that expressed by the divided characters in the novels.

The couple is the basic unit of the second radio play also: *6 810 000 litres d'eau par seconde* commissioned by Stuttgart radio as a stereophonic project. This time the distinction is made between groups by directional sound rather than by quality and Butor adds seven different volume levels which enable him to create a polyphony of voices from which certain words and sense patterns will stand out to create new and juxtaposed meanings within the dialogues of the various characters. The work is essentially an experiment with sound and with words as audible elements. It is constructed from many different layers, some of which can be eliminated at any time by a change in volume — the quieter passages disappearing or being covered by louder ones — hence the piece can be varied indefinitely.

In the background are street sounds and forest sounds supporting the present day commentary of the Speaker and the perpetual quotation from Chateaubriand's descriptions of Niagara by the Reader. Chateaubriand wrote two versions of his text, one in *Essai historique, politique et moral sur les révolutions anciennes et modernes considérées dans leurs rapports avec la Révolution française* (1797) and the other in *Atala, ou les amours de deux sauvages dans le désert* (1801). The inter-relation of the two versions, one fact, one fiction, as Butor uses them supports the structure of reality and dream in the characters' relationships with Niagara and with each other. The juxtaposition of past and present is of course that between Reader and Speaker.

Together with these sounds and voices are combined snatches of conversation. The characters are in couples at first, both members of each couple being heard through the same speaker, but gradually some of them separate in thought if not in body and hence are heard through different ones (Les Réveils, chapter VII). The characters change continually, but their types remain and others join them becoming more and more numerous, as lonely individuals are added to the different sorts of couple; the impression of a crowd as dense and as fluid as the water of the falls is produced. (By the end there are seventeen people included in the scene.)

A similar sense of motion is given by the passing time. As mentioned before, the play covers a year beginning in April, each scene showing a different month and each scene also incorporates one hour more than the preceding one so that there is a double movement like those in *L'Emploi du Temps* and later *Portrait de l'artiste en jeune singe.* The passage of the hours is marked by a Westminster chime which is, therefore, heard more and more frequently as the work continues, forcing the snatches of conversation and description to become more and more brief and staccato. A further element of haste is added by the very construction of the play. As it was not known how much time could be allowed for the performance Butor inserted within the scenes themselves a number of parentheses which can be included or omitted either to change the balance of the impression received or to expand or contract the play according to the needs of the radio programmer — no arbitrary truncation is then to be feared.

Niagara is a changing spectacle in itself. It is described by its changing patterns of flowers throughout the summer months. The colours are taken up again in the illumination of the falls in winter and each is a projection of the rainbows to be seen in the water itself. *6 810 000 litres d'eau par seconde,* although it certainly presents an American site as discussed above, is a pertinent study of the couple in a way made infinitely more mobile and hence both penetrating and ambiguous by the interweaving of the various conversations and commentaries. Above all, however, it is a pure description of the falls themselves. People are but specks in its history or drops in its river. The torrent of words, intermingling of sounds and increasing impression of speed throughout the play, beginning with its very title, turn the speakers of a stereophonic radio into the two halves of the falls themselves and force the listener into their presence. *6 810 000 litres d'eau par seconde* is the transmission of an experience within which words play a much more complex role than is usual in literature. Butor describes his text as having the form of a canon, each part of the text being divided into sections which are super-imposed while sections of other parts are interposed.[3]

For Butor a spectacle essentially contains music, a point he discusses at some length in "L'opéra c'est-à-dire le théâtre,"[4] and conversely music needs words.[5] Just as visual art is inseparable from language so is music; both are modified by it and modify it. In the radio plays Butor was able to experiment to a certain extent with oral-aural words. "Paysage de répons" (*Illustrations II*) was written in response to a composition by Henri Pousseur. *Votre Faust*, also in collaboration with Pousseur, is Butor's major attempt to unite text and music in spectacle to date.

Votre Faust[6] has six main characters, Henri the composer, the Director who asks Henri to write a Faust and offers to support him while he does so, no matter how long the project might take, Maggy, Henri's girl friend, Greta her sister, the Opera singer and Richard, Henri's friend. The Director makes his proposition to Henri in the first act and is the cause of Maggy being taken to prison. From then on what happens depends on the opinion of the audience who have first to vote on whether or not Maggy should be released and then later have opportunities to intervene and reverse their first decision. In the second part of the opera Greta is substituted for Maggy by the Director and the relationship may or may not prosper. Henri goes to the fair to see a performance of the old Faust puppet play and afterwards begins to travel. At the end Henri may or may not break his contract with the Director.

The structure of the opera turns on the visit to the Faust play. There the roles of the characters are clarified and so is the fact that they tend to be puppets in another's hands. Henri is identified with Faust though he remains in the audience (hence the real audience's participation is indicated too), Richard plays Faust's valet Guignol and Greta goes on stage to play Guignol's wife. All are masked. The Director arrives just in time to help Greta off the stage. It is evident that he is Mephistopheles.

This play provides a centre for a multi-level evocation of the whole of the Faust legend. Henri is continually surrounded by verbal, and allusive quotation from all other *Fausts*. We recognize Goethe's play in the story of Maggy, Thomas Mann's hero in Henri the musician. Marlowe is quoted in the original, Goethe in German and in Nerval's translation. Valéry's Faust and Lust are also there in the relationship established between the Devil and literature: the Director is responsible for Henri's libretto.

The characters move against a background of sound, words and music which comment on their actions. There are quotations from Offenbach (*Orphée aux Enfers* and *La Belle Hélène*), Donizetti (*Lucia di Lammermoor*), Wagner (*Tannhäuser*), Monteverdi (*Orpheo*) and Mozart (*Don Giovanni*), and we notice that all the operas have themes which reflect on the Henri-Maggy situation yet none of them treat *Faust* because Henri will not compose for such a theme. Simultaneously they evoke different periods, nationalities and styles of singing as Henri travels to Venice, Vienna, Naples, Mexico and New York (Goethe, *Faust* Part II). The evocation is completed for the audience by the projection of scenes and paintings (Rembrandt, Delacroix) on to screens at the back of the stage.

Butor's preoccupation with division within a character is treated

83

again here. The Faust theme is the treatment of man's need to choose between good and evil, wisdom and fame, and here it is shown in Henri's actions: he ceases to write church music when he begins his opera, he rejects Maggy, who sings in the Cabaret de l'Eglise (church cabaret) in favour of her sister Greta. (The two girls are played by the same actress so that the split is obvious.) The opera opens with Henri miming a lecture on modern music which is played on tape and then talking against his own voice about other preoccupations. Here the division is personal, but the act ends with the singing of a "Dies Irae" and a hymn to the Devil, intertwined and both in Latin — the dilemma has been shifted to a different level and as a result the intentions of the "Veniet Dominus" become ambiguous: Who is Lord? Latin is used for the moral problem in which Henri-Faust is trapped, while the multitude of modern languages used by the singers create another Babel — a situation which was after all the first Faustian challenge to the Almighty. (The use of these linguistic conventions recall *Description de San Marco*.)

The far-reaching effects of Faust's dilemma at all times are illustrated by the levels of the libretto. Butor has transposed the basic story into the twentieth century but provides it with many underlying levels: the old marionette plays, drama for live actors, opera, the story of Henri's life as shown on the stage, the audience's reaction to it and its close ties to the lives of Henri Pousseur and Butor himself.

The link between Henri the composer and Pousseur is firmly established by the fact that Pousseur wrote Henri's opening speech. Butor has likewise put himself in the place of the Director for he wrote the libretto. This conception of Butor's role is indicated by the title of the work: it is *Votre Faust*, Pousseur's and/or the audience's *Faust*, but not Butor's. He offers the choices but cannot control the decisions made during the course of the opera. The work is constructed in such a way that the audience must vote on which of the later acts it wishes to hear and has then four means of intervention to reverse its own decision. Twice a member of the audience is asked to say how he would like certain scenes to continue and twice the public is told that if it interrupts the action the scene will be re-enacted with a different conclusion.

Hence the audience must participate in Henri's progress and is included in Faust's dilemma. Salvation and damnation lie together in each man's hand. Should Henri choose love and humanity or fame? The audience is bombarded with information in mime,

84

poetry, music, images and scenes of daily life. It can see Henri's position more clearly than he can and thus must take decisions for him. The role the spectator chooses for himself depends on his conception of the world — will he perhaps become more aware of this if he takes part in *Votre Faust*? He will certainly be obliged to judge a situation.[7]

Butor demands of his audience what he demands of his reader: active participation. He creates situations, provokes questions and shows where information may be obtained — usually in books, buildings and works of art. He always brings in other people's work to enrich his own and increase the possible significance of both. The more the spectator, listener or reader knows about the works quoted the more he will understand the problems Butor tackles. Will Henri save Maggy from death? How strong is his love? Other legends are attached to the main theme to help solve the problems because nothing can be studied in isolation. Butor realizes that the use of one myth inevitably brings others to mind and he exploits the situation to prove to his audience that knowledge cannot be put into compartments. Orpheus (Offenbach, Monteverdi) symbolizes the supremacy of music even over death and the gods, and this new Faust that Butor offers is a musician. He gives power over Henri-Faust's destiny to the spectators too. Should he forget Maggy, break with the world, declare his intention to being his work and die? Or should he break his contract and go back to the beginning with Maggy's ghost? Like Orpheus he is offered a chance to start again.

Butor recreates the whole Faust legend and places his hero and audience in the middle of it. Simultaneously he teaches the story to his audience, makes them experience it, take responsibility for the result, and, if they wish to do so, identify the truths and problems it contains. Butor uses the legend as a vehicle for social criticism and for the stimulation of the traditional audience. *Votre Faust* is a total experience. It seems to depict the chaos of information which surrounds man and his struggle to survive within it. Butor's Faust and his audience become aware of the problems facing them in life, they see the choices offered and are free to choose. But will they ever understand the situation fully enough to make a right decision?

We see that for Butor theatrical presentations are essentially collaborative, expressive of shared experiences and common problems. Drama is a means of social communication offered to groups of people. Productions resemble sites and museums in that they incorporate a variety of presentations of their main theme. They are also

85

similar in their historical roots, their need for context and the number of people who have access to them. Sites, museums and dramatic spectacles are all created by a group for a group (the same or another). Contact is made between the two groups in a public situation in which the reaction of the groups within and between themselves can produce further development of the original topic, further understanding of the event presented.

An example of such a spectacle is the Indian dancing in *Où* (pp. 217-388). (We remember that Butor's chapter on "Spectacles" in *L'Arc* No. 39 begins with the Coptic liturgy and continues to the carnival in Rio.) Butor transforms a natural phenomenon (Niagara Falls) into a spectacle in *6 810 000 litres d'eau par seconde* and indicates that most of the people who were both part of the spectacle and watching it did not realize the significance of what they saw. Here we have a different attitude. The Zuni Indians have assimilated their world and formulated their beliefs about it. These they express in their dancing so that the spectacle is a ritual which encompasses an entire universe in its colours, its movements and masks. The cyclic repeat of the dances is a reaffirmation of that world, a sharing of belief for the Indians themselves, participants and dancers alike, and a key to understanding for the uninitiated spectators. Butor says that he learned about the ritual in class, in the Musée de l'Homme and in the Museum of the University of New Mexico. Now he must undergo the experience for himself. Like the Cambodian dances at Angkor, the ones at Zuni also take place at night, but this time they are not merely a tourist attraction; the Zuni tradition is still alive.

The dances are complicated and many years of initiation are needed before a complete understanding is reached. They go on all night and simultaneously in several houses in the Zuni village. The rite Butor attends is that of the midwinter solstice, a ritual of the affirmation of the stability of space and especially of the east, home of the rising sun. The dancers are painted and wear masks and feathers symbolic of their function. The principal colours are yellow, turquoise, red, white, multi-coloured and black representing north, west, south, east, the zenith and nadir respectively. (Formerly a Zuni house was built as a cube symbolic of the entire universe in the same way.)

The dancers representing the gods cross the river from outside the village and collect in the major house, that of Longhorn. He represents the path of the sun from dawn till dusk and the other chief gods are Pautiwa, god of the rising sun, and Shulawitsi,

86

heavenly fire (the household fire is called grandmother). With Longhorn waiting to welcome them are Shulawitsi's father and the Oracle, priest of the sun, Shulawitsi's parallel on earth. The gods dance the reaffirmation of the world, planting seeds and eating food.

At the same time in six other houses six Shalakos with their attendant warriors and servants act out the same ritual. This is interrupted from time to time by the "pumpkin-heads", ten clowns who parody the ritual in their own house. Then, leaving the first three among them, Father, Oracle and Archer, to continue their celebration the others go out two by two to disrupt the festivities of the Shalakos. They bear the names Bat, Little-eyes, Pout, Old Grandfather, the Joker, the Infant and Old Baby. They are shadows bearing the same relationship to men as men do to the gods. The Shalakos they try to disrupt are giants who link the world of men to the house of the universe. They come from outside the village at the beginning of the dance too.

Each house is decorated with symbols in the six colours of the universe and each dancer carries coloured seeds. In each house there are musicians and a choir who interact with the dancers and the main characters pronounce ritual speeches and responses. Here is a true spectacle by Butor's definition. It transmits and perpetuates the experience of a people who collaborate to bring it to pass. Expressive of an entire world view it incorporates all the arts (painting, dance, music, speech) within its pattern in such a way as to show quite clearly in all its complexity the relationship of man to his universe.

Any dramatic manifestation is the offering of experience and the seeking of response which will take the original subject nearer to its fulfilment. The Zuni Indians have a group belief to express in their own way; Butor and Pousseur try to create a similar experience within a European context in *Votre Faust*.

Likewise a lecture may be considered a spectacle of a specialized kind (again this is justified in *L'Arc*) but Butor treats most of his own as literature by republishing them in the volumes of *Répertoire*. One was created as an integral part of a concert, however, providing the text which turns the music into a spectacle by Butor's definition; this is *Dialogue avec 33 variations de Ludwig van Beethoven sur une valse de Diabelli*. Michel Butor was invited to lecture on the occasion of a rendering of the *Diabelli Variations*[8] and agreed to do so if he could insert his comments between the pieces of music in such a way as to create a dialogue between the lecturer and the

87

piano. Once the performance was over, he developed his text into a more complex system which then became the published work.[9]

The construction brings to mind that proposed by Charles Fourier and indeed the 32 rhumbs of *La Rose des Vents* are closely linked with the 33 variations (32 if the final minuet is considered a repeat of the original theme). The *Dialogue* divides the music, creating a pivot of variations 16 and 17, subdividing the work between 8 and 9, 24 and 25, hence dividing the 32 parts into 4 octaves, a major and a minor in each half. The four sections follow the four seasons and according to Butor's titles for them juxtapose town and country with public and private life. Within these four groups of eight variations are added eight interventions four on either side of the pivot.

Considering the pieces of music in groups of four, Butor gives them other titles, three for each piece, beginning with:

1 - 4 a) scenes of elegant life b) the nobility c) the palace.

He continues through scenes of bourgeois life, political life (equated with ruins!) ending with:

21 - 24 Scenes of bohemian life, fairies, the theatre
25 - 28 Scenes of deliverance, wise men, vines
29 - 32 Scenes of profound life, musicians, caverns.

Evidently the theatre and its use of the imagination is a close step from wisdom while music holds the highest place of all — a reflection on Faust, on the grottos of Pommersfelden and on Fourier with his world of Harmony. A further link with Fourier and *La Rose des Vents* is forged in a further series of titles where certain variations are given the attributes of the various ages of man: bronze age, copper, iron, silver, mercury leading to lead and plutonium together, the alchemists' base for gold and the scientists' base for the atomic age. As always we have a dichotomy and a choice.

The structure of *Dialogue* gives ever-widening possibilities to Beethoven's music. Glossary chapters (in italics) provide historical background and musical context and comparison with other composers. Next the titles of the variations suggest possibilities of interpretation on the human level (scenes from life) and the super-human (attribution of the names of planets to certain pieces), thus the imagination of the listener/reader is stimulated. The interventions give Butor's reaction to the music and his explanations of titles and structures implicit within and imposed upon the music. We notice that although Fourier and Beethoven tend to work in octaves, sixteens and thirty-twos, numbers suggested by music itself, Butor remains

88

faithful to his three and sevens, having this time a reverse of the structure of *Portrait de l'artiste en jeune singe*. The latter had three major sections one of which was subdivided into seven while *Dialogue* has groups of three within seven major divisions.

The groups of three are very evocative; first there is of course the 33 of the title, then the inter-relation of:

Beethoven	Fourier	Pousseur
Butor	Fourier	music
Butor	Pousseur	text/music

which resulted in new triads of:

Butor	text	Beethoven
Butor	text	Marcelle Mercenier (pianist)
Butor	text	audience

(The book would seem to evoke the dual relationship of the dialogue composer-pianist, author-reader, but when we begin to read *Dialogue* we realize that it contains one more element than usual: Beethoven *and* Butor demand our attention.) From the above comes a reconsideration of the Butor-text-Beethoven relationship which produces in its turn the final term:

text	reader	music

Within this process a profound change has taken place. *Dialogue* is no longer a spectacle but a subject for meditation. It has changed from a public statement requiring a public response within a given time to the expression of one dialogue — that between Butor and Beethoven — which gives birth to a new one; as well as the normal reader-author link a reader-composer is formed, inevitably transforming reader into listener and creating a dialogue on an aural plane as well as on a visual one. In both cases this is a private relationship expressed according to Butor in the *Diabelli Variations* themselves, for he writes:

On a souvent déclaré que les Diabelli défiaient l'interprétation, du moins l'interprétation publique; ... mais c'est qu'elles ne sont pas destinées premièrement au concert ... La notion d'*étude* ... destinée au solitaire qui travaille en chambre qui est son propre exécutant, son seul auditeur, succède à celle d'exercice destiné à préparer le virtuose, le musicien professionnel, à sa fonction dans la tribune de l'église ou du salon.[10]   (*Ed. G.*)

The music has become a basis for reflection, for study and for personal development. It is beginning to have a similar role to that of a book (a role whose importance has increased enormously since the advent of records and taped music). Indeed Butor continues:

Dès lors la façon dont le texte est écrit, presque indépendamment de la façon dont on pourrait l'entendre, acquiert une importance considérable.[11] (*Ed. G.*)

The *Diabelli Variations* contain Beethoven's vision as clearly as Fourier's writings contain his. In the presentation of both, in *Dialogue avec 33 variations de Ludwig van Beethoven sur une valse de Diabelli* and in *La Rose des Vents*, Butor acts as interpreter and catalyst, reducing a vast imagination to human level and using it to stimulate the minds of his readers. The movement of ritual discovered in the dance, transformed into drama and opera in the theatre, has become a private one with Butor in the self-assigned role of director controlling the stimulus.

We are left then to reflect upon the suggestions for study offered in *L'Arc*; the real rituals, dramatists and cinematographic topics:

1. Guillaume de Machaut
2. Rameau
3. Lope de Vega
4. The crowning of the Queen of England
5. XVI century triumphs
6. Aristophanes
7. Zeami
8. Lester Young
9. The Universal Exhibition
10. Cinema:
    1. Emile Cohl
    2. Griffith
    3. Buster Keaton
    4. Harry Langdon
    5. Witchcraft
    6. Murnau
    7. W. C. Fields
    8. Ivan the Terrible
    9. Anthony Mann
    10. John Cassavetes

which must then be juxtaposed to the imaginary spectacle for which they prepared the reader, so that he finds himself pushed back into the world of books and out into his own imagination with all the demands of production upon him. He is offered:

1. Pyramus and Thisbe in Shakespeare's *A Midsummer Night's Dream*.

2. The mime of Mick, Nick and the Maggies in James Joyce's *Finnegans Wake*.
3. The "pageant" in Virginia Woolf's *Between the Acts*.
4. *Love's Labours Lost* by Adrian Leverkuhn in Thomas Mann's *Dr. Faustus*.
5. Chaos Conquered in Victor Hugo's *The Man who Laughs*.
6. The puppet play in Cervantes' *Don Quixote*.
7. Wilhelm Meister's repertoire in Goethe's *Years of Apprenticeship*.
8. The grand theatre of Oklahoma in Kafka's *Amerika*.
9. The spectacle in Jean-Valentin Andreae's book *The Chemical Wedding of Christian Rosenkreuz*.
10. The Magic Box in Paul de Musset's *Mr. Wind and Mrs. Rain*.

Butor again takes part in the production and demands participation of his reader. The contributor editor of *L'Arc* No. 39 is the author-Director of *Votre Faust*, dancing the role of Shalako communicating the structures of the outer universe to the world of man.

Spectacles are collaborative performances, interpretive rituals which have a collective function reciprical to that of sites. In a given culture, each will reflect concerns and emphasis in comparable form. Each provides a structure for the expression of a group and is thus a knot in the network of historical and geographical relations. The reflective nature of Butor's writing is an image of the nature of its subject, a constant reminder of the dialectic between past and present, place and action, reality and imagination, and above all between groups and individuals by which the Western world has always expressed its concerns.

CHAPTER V: FOOTNOTES

[1] See also M. Spencer, "Architecture and poetry in *Réseau Aérien*," *The Modern Language Review*, 63, 1 (January 1968), pp. 57-65.

[2] "Influences de formes musicales sur quelques oeuvres," *Musique en jeu*, 4 (Paris: Editions du Seuil, 1971), p. 68: "The unity of identification is no longer the actor but the couple, but the same actor is heard in the first couple of both planes going to Nouméa, he constitutes a double character who divides himself up all around the world only to put himself together again at the end."

[3] *Ibid.*, p. 69.

[4] *L'Arc* No. 27 (1965), pp. 81-86, reprinted in *Répertoire III*, pp. 383-390.

[5] "Les mots dans la musique," *Musique en jeu*, 4, pp. 70-72.

6 Records: *Votre Faust*, 3 records, Harmonia Mundi 01 21580-6, Musique Nouvelle Ensemble, direction H. Pousseur, presentation Claude Micheroux. *Miroir de Votre Faust*, piano Marcelle Mercenier, WERGO 60039. Bibliography: *Votre Faust* in *La Nouvelle Revue Française* (Jan.-April 1962). H. Pousseur, *La Foire de Votre Faust* (Kassel: Bärenreiter-Verlag, 1968-69). J-Y Bosseur, *Votre Faust*, Cahier du Centre d'Etudes et de Recherches marxistes (1968). D. et J-Y Bosseur, "Elaboration de *Votre Faust*," *Musique en jeu*, 4, pp. 83-105.

7 In order to set up a similar dilemma for people who have the recorded version, Butor and Pousseur invented games to be played while listening to the opera (Plate 13). These games control progress across the records and thus, by shifting from variant to variant, change the destiny of the protagonists. The listener is in the grip of fate.

8 Marcelle Mercenier, pianist, 17th September, Autumn Festival, Liège 1970.

9 For a detailed history of the development of *Dialogue* see H. Pousseur, "Ecoute d'un dialogue," *Musique en jeu*, 4, pp. 73-82, and Appendix III for a plan of the work.

10 *Dialogue avec 33 variations de Ludwig van Beethoven sur une valse de Diabelli*, p. 23: "It has often been said that the Diabellis were very difficult to play, at least in public performance . . . but that is because they were not primarily intended for the concert hall. . . . The idea of an *étude* . . . destined for the pianist working alone in his room, his own performer, his own solitary listener, follows that of the exercise aimed at preparing the virtuoso, the professional musician, for his function in a church or salon."

11 *Dialogue*, p. 23: "Ever since, the way the text is written, almost independently of the way it may be heard, gains considerable importance."

CHAPTER VI

Livres[1]

In *Passage de Milan* Samuel Léonard and his friends discuss the analogical power of literature and its cumulative power as well as the danger of misinterpretation. They agree that if they were prepared to draw on a setting constructed in collaboration, each of their works could be used to deepen the significance of the others and would simultaneously profit from the pool of information offered to the reader. In spite of these advantages they are unable to bring themselves to do this as each author expresses himself through a different combination of times and places and cannot recognize himself in the others. A book is offered as a record of a personal experience within a world.

Revel's development in *L'Emploi du Temps* is based on his discovery of the detective story *Meurtre de Bleston* which leads him to explore Bleston in a certain way and to meet the author of the book. Subsequently he discusses the theory of the detective story with George Burton whose comments throw light on Revel's situation and on the role of the author. His theory is that every detective novel is based on two murders, the original one committed by the criminal and the legal one committed by the detective in punishing the murderer.

When murder is committed the detective must reconstruct in every detail the events leading up to the crime in order to be in possession of the whole truth and commit the second murder which should restore coherence and balance. Hence a person must question the motivation of the act he performed and recapture his past completely so that he may be able to understand it fully. Then he will be capable of acting a second time in a reasonable and accurate fashion.

The second killing is in fact caused by the revelation of the truth and is prefigured by the crime. It is an action necessary to obliterate the stain caused by the first one. Only a complete and fixed view of the past can give the qualification for coherent action in the future. Revel is searching for this totality and so he writes his book, but he fails to achieve what he wants, not only because human memory is a subjective instrument but because information is irregularly available. Burton yearns for the same end and so creates it artificially in his books. The use of the detective novel shows that man cannot gain possession of truth while he is in the flux of time, for this kind of story deals only with a period which has a definite final moment — that of the crime — and it cannot be influenced by present happenings.

Burton postulates that the detective is son of Oedipus. Both solve the obvious riddle and gain the reward, yet they do so by killing the person to whom they owe their title and existence: Oedipus slew his father, the detective is responsible for the death of the criminal without whom he could not exist. This connection between Oedipus and the detective also joins them to the artist for he must sacrifice his predecessor in order to put forward his own values for society. Burton then represents one generation of artists and Revel the following one, for Revel is responsible for Burton's accident. Revel links Oedipus with Theseus because each killed his father and burned his own city. He identifies with Theseus who went to Crete to avenge the deaths of Athenian youths, hence he assumes the detective's role, but from this resulted other deaths, not only that of the Minotaur but of his father and so he finds himself first playing detective then criminal.

The sequence is illustrated in *L'Emploi du Temps* and reflected in *Meurtre de Bleston*. When he wrote *Meurtre de Bleston* Burton wished to expose the fratricide of which he was sure Richard Tenn was guilty. The author of the detective story was playing detective himself as well as writing about one. Revel in his turn denounces Burton as the detective following Tenn, while he himself is trying to find the identity of the man who tried to kill Burton. He also denounces his own faults: the betrayal of Burton, his treatment of Anne and Rose. This is a theme which recurs in *Degrés*: the artist is necessarily apart from the world searching for the truth it is hiding from him and as a result the people around him suffer. Then he who is responsible for their suffering becomes victim in his turn, the criminal awaiting retribution. Revel thus joins Oedipus, Theseus and Cain, all murderers marked by fire, and like them he also escapes to profit from his experience and maybe solve the mystery at a later date.

The detective novel introduces Revel to his surroundings and also provides him with a method for dealing with the experience he gains there. He must look back through time for the key to the future and he must write down what he learns to fix it for the future. Here we have the dual role of literature as Butor sees it.

In 1960 Butor published two books which are the theory and practice of this belief: *Répertoire* and *Degrés*. *Répertoire* contains twenty-one essays of which the first and the last direct the reader's attention to Butor's purpose. The other nineteen at first glance are very interesting studies of movements, individual works and authors. If we are aware of Butor's attitude to books, however, we soon realize that the essays are illustrations in a historical sequence of the theory proposed in the first, "Le roman comme recherche". In this essay man is shown to gain his first grasp on reality by means of the stories he is told as a child. As he grows, literature takes over this function and presents experience (or possible experience) in a clearly structured fashion in which the analogies can be seen easily. As man's situation is changing all the time the form in which this situation can be transmitted must be modified also, hence the development of ways of storytelling. The previous forms of the novel cannot encompass today's world so new forms have to be found which show what is lacking in the old ones. Butor writes:

... il est évident que la forme étant un principe de choix ... des formes nouvelles révéleront dans la réalité des choses nouvelles, des liaisons nouvelles et ceci naturellement, d'autant plus que leur cohérence interne sera plus affirmée par rapport aux autres formes, d'autant plus qu'elles seront plus rigoureuses.[2] (*Ed. M.*)

The novel reveals a new reality from which must spring a new novel form which can provide tools to deal with the new reality. We see that the role given to the detective-author in *L'Emploi du Temps* is elaborated, for the text continues:

La recherche de nouvelles formes romanesques le pouvoir d'intégration soit plus grand, joue donc un triple rôle par rapport à la conscience que nous avons du réel, de dénonciation, d'exploration et d'adaptation. Le romancier qui se refuse à ce travail, ne bouleversant pas d'habitudes, n'exigeant de son lecteur aucun effort particulier, ne l'obligeant point à ce retour sur soi-même, à cette mise en question de positions depuis longtemps acquises, a certes, un succès plus facile, mais il se fait le complice de ce profond malaise, de cette nuit dans laquelle nous nous débattons. Il rend plus raides encore les réflexes de la conscience, plus difficile son éveil, il contribue à son étouffement, si bien que, même s'il a des intentions généreuses, son oeuvre en fin de compte est un poison.[3]
(*Ed. M.*)

The formal structures of a novel are thus means to a greater realism. The rest of *Répertoire* provides an examination of the forms and styles necessary to the transmission of this reality at different times, and the evolution from one period to another. "L'alchimie et son langage" which proves to hold the key to *Portrait de l'artiste en jeune singe* initiates the reader into levels of meaning and the care with which a text must be studied. "Sur le *Progrès de l'Ame* de John Donne" reinforces the author's search for unity in himself and his means of symbolic expression. (Here we find the possible origin of the Cain symbol in *L'Emploi du Temps.*) Through his commentary on the authors who have interested him Butor teaches his reader how to read a work properly, with full attention and active awareness of every detail. We begin to realize that things do not simply "happen" in good novels, they are demanded by circumstances, circumstances which imposed themselves upon the author in such a way that he had to elucidate them to his own satisfaction — hence Butor's author-heroes, and his statement that literature provides society with a kind of laboratory within which it can experiment on methods of seizing its reality.

The social role Butor attributes to the novel is thus explained at the beginning of *Répertoire*; at the end of the same volume he writes of his personal need of such a form:

Je n'écris pas des romans pour les vendre, mais pour obtenir une unité dans ma vie; l'écriture est pour moi une colonne vertébrale; et pour reprendre une phrase d'Henry James: "Le romancier est quelqu'un pour qui rien n'est perdu".

Il n'y a pour le moment de forme littéraire dont le pouvoir soit aussi grand que celui du roman. On peut y relier d'une façon extrêmement précise, par sentiment ou par raison, les incidents en apparence les plus insignifiants de la vie quotidienne, et les pensées, les intuitions, les rêves en apparence les plus éloignés du langage quotidien.

Il est ainsi un prodigieux moyen de se tenir debout, de continuer à vivre intelligemment à l'intérieur d'un monde quasi furieux qui vous assaille de toutes parts.[4]

The author then writes in order to keep a hold on his environment and what he writes helps the reader to do likewise. The latter should then react in his turn, becoming aware of his situation, reacting within it and hence producing a new reality as feedback to the writer; the chain is endless. Considered in this way books are essential to man, being his major means of learning from others, exploring for himself and teaching the human situation in all its complexity.

Degrés is Butor's illustration of this. The novel is set in a school, concerned with the boys and their teachers, the presentation and learning of lessons. Books are expected in this setting and so could be easy to ignore, but *Degrés* is built entirely on the texts studied, on other authors, other traditions, other periods. Through these the reader will come to understand the relationship between Pierre Vernier and his nephew Pierre Eller and also the aims Vernier has for his pupils, his belief in discovery and the multiple possibilities of the world.

The texts studied by the boys of IIA and also IA, Pierre Eller's brother's class, are quoted throughout *Degrés* but they are used for a different purpose in each section of the novel, and the key to the structure is not offered explicitly to the reader until he reaches the last one. In the first section in the book the curriculum for the coming academic year is listed and the texts are mentioned at intervals because Vernier intends to read them all in order to follow the class he is describing in fields other than his own. It is easy to consider them as an integral part of the classroom situation and hence as unworthy of special attention, but indication that this is not the case is given by one lesson which is explored in detail: Vernier's opening class on the discovery of the New World. By means of historical fact he hopes to convey to the boys an awareness of the infinite realm of possibility open to them in life. He stimulates their realization by the juxtaposition of texts drawn from Marco Polo's visit to China and Montaigne's essay *Des Coches*. Neither of them seem directly relevant to the basic history lesson at first, yet they give a real understanding of the spirit of the age.

Butor has shown how his novel is to be read, albeit obliquely. In the second section the boys studying the texts will apply them tentatively to their own situation, and in the third section Henri Jouret will use them quite openly to draw analogies with the story of Vernier's relations with Eller and the class. Any reader who has not been drawing his own conclusions until this point will see quite clearly the way Butor intends them to be used. The characters make use of certain works in a limited fashion but the reader can go much further in his analogy and thus fill out the sparse information available to create more detailed relationships and characters in the round.

Each reader creates his own novel according to the extent of his knowledge of the texts mentioned. Ignorance of one work or lack of detail in his memory of another will leave him with a different picture of the events from that obtained by someone with an acute awareness of all that Butor offers. The book is constructed from personal experience as the barrier dividing the different authors and centuries are broken down and the resources of literature are applied to life. As always the person with the greatest knowledge, depth of awareness and flexibility will understand most clearly what is happening. As in life there is no solution, no definite interpretation. The reader must make an effort to perceive and correlate information. Butor hopes that the novel will modify first reading habits, then thought patterns and finally the attitude to life of his readers. *Degrés* is an attack on the rigidity of convention and habit.

The texts have two functions in the novel: to enable the reader to increase his understanding of the characters and their personal situation and to create a realization of the vast possibilities open to man in the world today. Although, at first glance, the choice of texts seems to consist of the usual school selection, each work throws light on some aspect of the two main themes, progress and the Eller-Vernier saga, and also, in retrospect, on the aim of education itself, which is surely to create an understanding of the world and its people from as many different aspects as possible.

Vernier plans a lesson on the voyages of discovery, those to the New World in particular. The lesson is to be the focal point of the book he is writing because through it he is hoping to change his pupils' outlook on life. The discoverers freed themselves from the geographical boundaries of mediaeval Europe at a time when restrictions in all realms — philosophy, religion, art, and education — were being rejected, man was reconsidering every aspect of life and the whole outlook was changing. The supreme examples of achievement that had previously been beyond the realm of the imagination were the marvels of the court of China as revealed by Marco Polo and the discovery of a new continent. To show this state of mind as clearly as possible Vernier reads extracts from Polo's description of the palace of the Great Khan and from Montaigne's essay *Des Coches* which begins: "Nostre monde vient de découvrir un autre (et qui nous respond si c'est le dernier de ses frères ...)."[5] [*sic*]

Preparing his lesson and his book Vernier finds that he is discovering a new world himself, looking at everything around him in a very different way. His own life has become a voyage from which Eller should profit. This was after all the way Columbus read and annotated Marco Polo's writings before setting out himself to discover greater things and it is the way the reader of *Degrés* should be stimulated into criticism, thought and action as a result of the novel.

(We see the same movement from artist to successor as in *L'Emploi du Temps*.)

Life as a voyage is an idea reflected in the Classical texts read by IIA. Beginning with the *Odyssey* and the *Aeneid*, the thrill of a quest with all its hardships and pleasures is presented to the boys, but gradually discovery becomes conquest and Hannibal is described crossing the Alps, Verrès pillaging Sicily. Man's inability to cope with great achievement, the baseness of his nature and his personal greed outweigh the glory and honour of the original intention.

This is not the side of things that Vernier wishes to show to his pupils, however, and he reads only the sections of Montaigne's work which marvel at the vast opportunities of life. But it is not the only aspect of which the reader of *Degrés* will be aware. Should he consider the text either with respect to the New World or to the twentieth century he will think of the whole of Montaigne's essay. The rest of *Des Coches* bewails the evils of the Conquistadors, the viciousness of their nature and the havoc they wreak among ignorant but naturally virtuous people whom they should have instructed to become the successors and surpassers of European civilization (again the idea of pushing forward into the future). Montaigne blames the corruption of education for the wickedness, an idea which plunges into the heart of the revolution of his time and ours.

To draw an analogy between the Renaissance and the twentieth century would seem a valuable exercise. The Renaissance is the epitome of Vernier's ideal of the discovery of the world, wonder and advance. The boys study this in their French classes, but the same texts illuminate the weakness and wickedness of human nature, considerations which Vernier refuses to take into account but which the pupils must learn from other sources if they are to have more successs in life than their teacher. The gulf between idealism and wisdom is manifest in the ideas on education expressed by Rabelais who is desirous of grasping all that learning has to offer, wanting to make every man "un abîme de science", and those of Montaigne who was writing a generation later in realization of the incapacity of the human mind to encompass the vastness of universal knowledge. As a result he turns to individuality and wants to form the mind, not fill it. The educational system was no longer suitable to the society in which it functioned and so had to be changed. Is Butor criticizing the French system or proving its relevance to his work?

IIA study the above ideas and many others centring on the sixteenth century. In *Degrés* the theories of the authors are put into a wider perspective for the reader by brief references to history lessons incorporating the major political, religious, artistic and ideological upheavals of the time. Freedom from the constraint represented by the Middle Ages is the aim; a rediscovery of ancient literature (tightening the web of *Degrés* by linking the periods) provokes an exploration of the mind; a new and personal consideration of religious doctrine and literature, of morals and philosophy, coincides with the voyages of discovery and creates a fresh vision of the world and its future. This is why so much stress is placed on the Renaissance in *Degrés*. Containing so clearly everything that Vernier is trying to achieve in the present, study of this period adds innumerable facets to his words, illustrates the multiplicity of possibility, leads the mind on with every reference, however trivial, towards yet another horizon to be conquered.

Even this last sentiment finds its expression in a text which adds to the original surge of emotion, a sonnet by Keats, "On first looking into Chapman's Homer". In the poem the glories of Classical literature are joined with the marvellous discovery of the Pacific Ocean by Cortez and his men who

> Looked at each other with a wild surmise
> Silent upon a peak in Darien.

A new realm of possibility was open before them.

Texts link to form a picture which becomes more and more vast, joining marvel with corruption in an overwhelming desire to advance, to search for wider, more accurate knowledge — a compulsion which grips Vernier's pupils, tugs at his readers and drags him to his death, worn out by the struggle for universal and detailed comprehension of his surroundings, victims of the trap of the Rabelaisian conception of education.

The second group of texts, instead of putting forward Vernier's aim to chart the school year so that his nephew may learn from it and be able to travel beyond his uncle's world, enables Butor to present an unusual picture of his main characters and their situation. Neither described by an omniscient author, nor seen through the restricted vision of one of the protagonists, the relationship between Vernier and Eller is developed by the reader through the texts. The facts fit into every literary work mentioned in *Degrés* and each one offers additional detail to the original story, presenting the feeling between uncle and nephew from one angle and then from another. No definite interpretation is selected. The possibilities are endless and vary according to the amount and depth of realization and knowledge of each reader; the book is constructed from each reader's experience. The personalities of Vernier and Eller are there to be discovered by each reader according to his ability, should he be prepared to make a similar effort to that required in the perception of the outside world.

Certain extracts of authors already mentioned fit into this category too, notably the letter from Gargantua to Pantagruel. The *Aeneid* is the story of the journey to a new land where Aeneas' descendants can go on to further greatness — Vernier's ideal, already linked with the relationship between Columbus and Marco Polo. Passages concerning Ulysses and Nausicaa, and Aeneas and Dido, illuminate another side of Pierre Vernier — his personal life. He loves Micheline Pavin but will not or cannot abandon his book to settle down with her. She gives him all the help and encouragement she can and, like Nausicaa, accepts his desertion with patience. At least that is the outward appearance, but the shadow of Dido remains and with it the possibility of despair and suicide.

Pierre Eller is thrilled by the responsibility of working with his uncle. For him the discovery texts take on a double glory. So does the history of cruelty which brings persecution and death in its wake when his classmates turn against him and he suffers deception at the hands of his uncle whom he trusts. Caesar's cry "Help me Cassius or I drown" is Vernier's appeal for his aid and Vernier, like Caesar, is god at this time. Like Caesar too he abandons his friend. Marot's *Epistre à Lyon Jamet* iterates the same call for help. Marot once saved his friend's life and is now in prison himself asking to be freed. It is clear that Vernier is trapped in his desire to write and cannot manage without Eller's help.

The relationship between uncle and nephew, and the character of each, is merely outlined in *Degrés*, but references echo through the school work to give wider implications, greater depth and precision to the evolution of their story, to the change in Vernier, Eller's escape and his future profit. To this end four plays are used in great detail, two by Racine, two by Shakespeare. The more extensive the knowledge of these works, the more exact the analogy that can be drawn from them, but the passages quoted are sufficient to show the possibilities and to give the key to an awakened desire to know more.

Macbeth outlines the plot, the struggle between Vernier the author and Uncle Pierre. Macbeth and Banquo meet the witches who promise immediate greatness to Macbeth but continued glory to Banquo's descendants. Vernier the author is personified in Macbeth; his human side as uncle then takes the role of Banquo, sacrificed to Macbeth's increased power. From being content to write for his nephew's benefit, Vernier comes to desire fame for himself. Micheline Pavin encourages him to write, so she must figure as Lady Macbeth. Eller is represented by Banquo's son Fleance who narrowly escapes slaughter at the same hand as his father and who will live to profit from the turn of events. Vernier's death is thus shown as a direct result of his desire for fame — a rather different presentation from his own idealistic statements.

Iphigénie tells the story of a sacrifice essential to progress. The Greek fleet cannot set sail for Troy until Agamemnon has sacrificed his daughter Iphigénie to the gods. Previously he has promised her to Achille, but he is certain that the young man's allegiance to his superior (Agamemnon himself) and his impatience for war will outweigh any feeling he might have for the girl. Unexpectedly it does not, and Achille shows himself ready to abandon his aspirations for love of the girl. Seeing this Eriphile, whom Achille captured and who is in love with him, offers herself in Iphigénie's stead. A reader of *Degrés* has the possibility of making the following substitutions: Vernier-author plays Agamemnon, Eller becomes Achille and Iphigénie, the unfortunate victim, is the personification of an abstraction — Eller's relationship with his class. When his school friends threaten to turn against him, because they think he is spying for his uncle, Eller abandons all collaboration in Vernier's book. (We notice that literature is as disruptive as war.) Eriphile who dies of unrequited love is thus the role left for the Uncle Pierre side of Vernier. Such an interpretation suggests an over-possessive fondness for his nephew on the part of Vernier. This is an aspect not previously indicated to the reader, but which is confirmed by Jouret's description of the death-bed scene where Vernier has eyes for no one but Pierre.

So far the plays treated have been ones read by classes other than IIA and thus present the events as they might be seen and interpreted by an outsider. From one angle Vernier would be considered over-ambitious for literary fame — the artist making his near ones suffer as he struggles to reveal the whole of society to itself — from another as an overly loving uncle. The last point is supported by mention of Molière's *Ecole des Femmes* in which Vernier may be cast as Arnolphe, the adoring old man who is trying to form his nephew. In both cases the result is the same: the young person turns to a contemporary, leaving the old man to suffering which is no less real for being unreasonable.

Eller's class is reading *Britannicus*. They see Vernier as Néron, "un monstre naissant", and Eller as Britannicus, his fifteen-year-old victim. However, it is possible to show a much more detailed analogy if Britannicus is played by Uncle Pierre, killed by Néron-Vernier-author. Again the power of creation is proved dangerous to the person it controls and everyone around him. Narcisse is the desire to write which exercises such a deadly influence over Britannicus and Burrhus is the rational side of Vernier when he decides to write. His reason recognizes the difficulties and dangers and tries to prevent the course of events. Agrippine, who is kept at a distance until Britannicus is dead, symbolizes Micheline Pavin who encourages Vernier-author to begin to write. Junie is Pierre Eller, young and virtuous. Néron's proposal then becomes Eller's involvement in Vernier's project, and Britannicus' death the violent rupture of the uncle-nephew relationship. Junie escapes Néron and "sans mourir elle est morte pour lui."[6] She always loves Britannicus as Eller cherishes the memory of his fond uncle when faced with Vernier his teacher. As for Vernier, his book looses its impetus and begins to collapse when Pierre has gone. His feeling is deep, though misplaced, and may be summed up in the closing lines of the play where the possibility of suicide reflects on Vernier's illness.

Julius Caesar is the Shakespeare play on the curriculum and it is concerned almost exclusively with Vernier's character which matches that of Cassius to a surprising degree. Applied to Vernier by most of the characters in *Degrés* are the lines:

> Yon Cassius has a lean and hungry look.
> He thinks too much: such men are dangerous.   (I, ii)

the speech continues:

> Yet if my name were liable to fear
> I do not know the man I should avoid
> So soon as that spare Cassius. He reads much
> He is a great observer, and he looks
> Quite through the deeds of men . . .
> Seldom he smiles and smiles in such a sort
> As if he mocked himself and scorn'd his spirit
> That could be moved to smile at anything.
> Such man as he be never at heart's ease
> Whiles they behold a greater than themselves,
> And therefore are they very dangerous.

So much of this speech is contained in descriptions of Vernier in *Degrés* that the rest becomes acceptable to the reader, without question, and Vernier seems a harder and more ambitious man than previously suspected. Caesar, the man who has even more power after his death than before, is represented by the book which haunts Vernier, and Caesar's murder by the moment when he begins to write it. Vernier walks about Paris during the night of Eller's birthday and finally phones Micheline Pavin to announce his decision to begin. Likewise Cassius walked abroad during the storm which foretold Caesar's death declaring:

> Cassius from bondage will deliver Cassius

and this he intended to do by his "strength of spirit." Cassius is obsessed with Caesar. In the storm he saw the danger to the great man but not to himself though he, like Vernier, dies as a result of the murder.

Eller plays the part of Brutus who did the deed for his friend and loved him. As in each of the other texts he is portrayed as virtuous and honest, faithful to his friends and true in his affections. Vernier is writing his book to show a description of Eller aged fifteen to an older Eller. Cassius had a similar aim when he said:

> And since you know you cannot see yourself
> So well as by reflection, I your glass
> Will modestly discover to yourself
> That of yourself which you yet know not of.   (I, ii)

After the murder Brutus and Cassius are together against the forces of Caesar's friends. The people turn against Cassius at the time when, unknown to him, Brutus is suffering from the news of the death of his wife. They quarrel and their words express the feelings of Vernier and his nephew when Eller, smarting from his friends' criticism, breaks with his uncle (IV, iii). This is the beginning of the end for Vernier and the disillusioned Cassius. Everything goes wrong and Cassius kills himself at a moment when appearances give an erroneous idea of his failure in battle. Vernier too is killed by a distortion of the truth and a certainty of failure. Alike in life, they could share the same epitaph:

> Mistrust of good success hath done this deed,
> O hateful Error, Melancholy's child,
> Why dost thou show to the apt thoughts of men
> The things that are not? O Error, soon conceiv'd
> Thou never com'st unto a happy birth,
> But kill'st the mother that engender'd thee.   (IV, vi)

Caesar is the most comprehensive of the textual analogies, filling out Vernier's character in a remarkable fashion.

Other aspects of the situation are indicated by the plays mentioned briefly as future studies for IIA. *Cinna* shows the tensions working on Eller and Vernier, as either could be cast in the role of Auguste who was betrayed by the person he trusted. Similarly both could take the title part since they are torn by divided loyalties. Such ambiguity adds a richness to the characters in *Degrés* which could never be obtained by direct narration. *Polyeucte* shows Vernier sacrificing himself for an ideal — an interpretation which is closer to his alleged motives. Then this idea is counter-balanced by *Tartuffe* in which he is shown as a hypocrite, exploiting his fond nephew (Orgon) although everyone else can see his intentions.

The situation between Eller and Vernier is ambiguous. Presented normally it would perforce be simpler, less intriguing. Offered to the reader through the texts it has the very human quality of the not-quite-known, hence inviting speculation.

The works used so far have been taught to the boys either by Vernier himself or by Eller's other uncle, Henri Jouret, teacher of French and Classics, friend and confidant of the protagonists, and they have dealt only with the main theme of *Degrés*. Each of the remaining books applies to the personal situation of the person teaching it as well as to the Vernier-Eller relationship. M. Bonnini, teacher of Italian, reads Dante with his pupils. The pieces selected are a sonnet from the *Vita Nuova*, "Inferno" and "Purgatorio" from the *Divina Commedia*. Beatrice represents M. Bonnini's wife who is ill and dying. The sonnet "Tanto gentile et tanto onesta pare" expresses his love for her, the "Inferno" the time of her illness when he knows that she will die and "Purgatorio" the sublimation of her memory while awaiting his own death. It may also be assumed that Beatrice represents Vernier's aim and that the poem in her honour is his idealization of his work. He sees himself as Virgil leading Dante through all the perils up to paradise, then watching him go further than he can himself. Dante is Eller of course and Beatrice is the finished work which will help him because of the love he had for her.

M. Bailly, the English master, is the other teacher closely connected with IIA. His marriage is breaking up and he has a mistress, Claire, with whom he dreams of starting a new life. When his divorce is granted, however, he tastes freedom as a single man once more, he realizes that life is full of possibilities and it is implied that he will not marry her. She has become one of the "realms of gold" which the traveller in Keats' "On first looking into Chapman's Homer" crossed before reaching the "peak in Darien" which changed everything.

His class reads Coleridge's "Rime of the Ancient Mariner." This poem is the corner-stone of the whole textual edifice because, as well as reflecting Bailly's life with his wife Elizabeth, it contains both an analogy of the situation between Vernier and Eller and also the theme of discovery discussed above.

For Bailly marriage was his voyage and the death of the albatross the end of his love for Elizabeth. The responsibility for his family was still round his neck, however, until the decision to divorce. Being won by the woman, presumably Claire, he was obliged to live in a house where he was disliked until the separation was effected and he was free again, though he would always bear the scar of his first marriage.

The poem also forms an allegory of the main story: Vernier is symbolized by the mariner and the Pierre Eller for whom the book is being written is the wedding guest, who learns from the mariner's experience. The school year and the writing of the book are represented by the voyage, and as Pierre Eller helps this on its way, he plays the part of the albatross. Eller's classmates are the sailors. They dislike the boy's connection with his uncle, but as all appears to go well at first they accept the situation. Then the book ceases to advance, all the suspicions are aroused again, shared this time by the boys and teaching staff. However, Eller remains faithful to Vernier (the bird around his neck). As the game of dice separates the crew from the mariner, so Vernier is cut off from everyone around him by his writing. The mariner's unconscious prayer symbolizes the tactless and inopportune remark of Vernier's which provokes Eller's departure from the class and the rupture of their relationship. Lessons continue just as the ship moves on, worked by the dead, and like the mariner Vernier falls ill. The voices he hears are those of the family talking about his work. Before the end of the year Vernier is back at work but he cannot finish his project. Henri Jouret who finishes writing the book is thus the pilot. The pilot's boy goes mad from the shock of seeing the mariner and this is a final comment on the effect of events on Pierre Eller.

M. Jouret terminates the project Vernier began. He is the outside observer giving an objective view of the events. Hence the texts he teaches are Montesquieu's *Lettres Persanes* and Saint-Simon's

Mémoires. The Criticism of the Revocation of the Edict of Nantes gives an insight into Jouret's disapproval of the dangerous situation in which Eller finds himself, and also into his knowledge that Vernier, like Louis, failed to realize the suffering he was causing. It also suggests that Eller's rejection of his uncle was an attempt to effect a public reconciliation with his class-mates and was in no way a disavowal of the affection and esteem he felt for Vernier. Observation of the court at the death of the Dauphin (Saint-Simon) shows the keen watch Jouret kept on his class and the insight he has into their affairs. They rejoiced at Vernier's downfall but Eller regrets it, just as the Duc d'Orléans unexpectedly wept for the man who had been kind to him.

The boys of IIA read other things than school books and their choice of reading matter adds its own contribution to the various impressions of events. They pass among themselves the science-fiction magazines *Fiction* and *Galaxie*. It is unfortunate that the October 1954 issues of these journals are no longer readily available to the reader of *Degrés* since the interpretations they offer are as rich as any provided by the classical texts. *Wolves don't cry* supports the image of a hard, wolf-like Vernier, set apart from the rest of his kind by his different reaction to his surroundings. It connects with the Cassius analogy and also with the figure of the North African who recurs at intervals throughout *Degrés*.

In *Jeu de Silence* a soldier is controlled by a higher power by means of a tiny radio and bomb inserted into his brain. He and the girl who saves him have to carry out their plan in silence to avoid it being found out and the soldier killed. The boys think Eller is the soldier, Vernier the controller, while Eller sees himself as the secret helper of his uncle and revels in the excitement of the game. His change of attitude shows clearly as time goes on, illustrated by the titles *Quelque chose pour rien* and *Dis-moi qui tu hantes*;[7] disillusioned he may be, but he cannot rid himself of his uncle's influence.

Events have been shown from all angles through the many texts incorporated into *Degrés*, expanding the ideas, weaving connections and developing character. Towards the end of the book this becomes much more obvious as Butor gives the key of his work to the reader. References multiply and as the book progresses one word evokes a whole panorama of implications. Nor does the reader escape criticism; the "passionnante brochure illustrée gratuite" entitled *On vous jugera sur votre culture*[8] is not mentioned by accident. Butor is ready to teach his readers, but he demands their full co-operation and a great deal of effort, for there is little comment on the texts during the course of *Degrés*. They are quoted in class, translated for homework, but it is the responsibility of the reader to put the passages to the most profitable use his knowledge will allow, restricting the novel to the superficial story or enlarging it in his own way to fill out the characters and build around them a panoramic vision of man's aspirations and possibilities.

Degrés draws on the totality of knowledge amassed from all previous reading and it applies the realizations so formed to the perception of daily life. A diligent reader of the novel becomes vitally aware of the interaction between the world of literature and the one in which he moves, especially in the realm of human judgment. When properly appreciated the novel fulfils Butor's aim to change the attitude of the reading public by decreasing significantly the gulf which frequently divorces experience read from experience lived. It stimulates close attention to a text and proves that a critical reading of one work has repercussions in the pleasure and knowledge obtained from another. The books Butor reads are projections from the ones he writes, those he writes are born of those he has read. The book is the link between man and reality. Hence it is not surprising that all his creations, as we have seen already, have their roots in one or more texts which are essential to the structure of the new work and also create a dialogue within it. It is clear also that Butor's critical methods, when applied to his own work, produce extremely rich results.

Awareness, information and imagination are the elements necessary to a reader, and these Butor manifests in all his work. Thus in *Histoire Extraordinaire* a study of Baudelaire develops from a letter he wrote describing a dream, and all the dreams in Butor's work past and future are given added importance. *Histoire Extraordinaire* offers, together with *Degrés*, a key to *Portrait de l'artiste en jeune singe* — a work built on influence, dream and quotation. But then Butor's works are interwoven so tightly that every one throws light on the others and expands the world he offers to his reader. His study of Baudelaire shows how an author's mind can synthesize a life with all its influences, aspirations and actions into a deceptively simple sequence which must be broken down and analysed to be appreciated in its true density. In *Essais sur les Essais* Butor displays to the reader how an author's work becomes more complex and multi-layered as he writes. Montaigne uses quotation liberally and therefore must be of interest to Butor who, in studying the *Essais*, teaches his reader once more how his own works should be read. He who recognizes several series of quotations will have a different impression of what he has read than he who only knows one of the authors quoted. The arrangement of quotations and their position within the new work produce repercussions which demand fresh thought — and in the author as much as in the reader.

Butor shows us how Montaigne withdraws gradually from the world around him to become absorbed in his writing which in turn becomes his inner world and his description of the world outside. It is his preparation for death. In both Baudelaire and Montaigne we find a tremendous will to write, a belief in the power of literature to smooth their path in the world. For both there is a link between their literature and imminent death. Proust (*Les Sept Femmes de Gilbert le Mauvais*) also shares these preoccupations. Writing brings understanding and gives immortality, for an author's ideas are fixed in his book and are developed through the ages by succeeding authors. We have seen this already in Butor's fictional characters and here his belief is shared and substantiated by "authorities". Rabelais, the fourth author to whom Butor has given considerable study, supports this idea. For him too literature and death have a close connection, but not a personal one like that of the authors mentioned previously; Rabelais ran the risk of execution for the ideas he wrote in his books. In all cases the proximity of death gave impetus to creation. Rabelais was forced to multiply some of his inventions as disguise and protection against censure and persecution, hence his reader must decipher his work for himself. Montaigne likewise increased the number and variety of his quotations, mixing authority and "trompe l'oeil" for authority. Theirs is a world of appearance and underlying significance. Proust painted a world of masks and surfaces too, and so did Baudelaire, but both in a spirit of condemnation. All of them seek a "golden age", a utopia, a Harmony. Montaigne and Rabelais search for it through their exploration of the wisdom of the ancients which they will use to push into the future. Proust finds his salvation within the work of art itself while Butor's projection of Fourier in *La Rose des Vents* is the inevitable accomplishment of the utopian dream where the system creates its own end. Baudelaire is associated with Fourier by reference; *Histoire Extraordinaire* is built on Fourier's pattern of sixteen chapters and the author is referred to several times. The juxtaposition of Mme Aupick and Jeanne, General Aupick and Poe, give ascending and descending male and female movements, while the treatment of the education of children

(Poe's school-life — the dream gallery), food (wine-drugs) and higher education follow Fourier's development. Education and experience bring harmony at first and hence the optimistic tone of Rabelais and Montaigne, but for Poe, Baudelaire and Proust it brings malady and death. The works themselves now become the ascendant and descendant series in their turn. Baudelaire is the true Cain-figure of denunciation, destruction and progress we have seen in *L'Emploi du Temps* and which we find at the end of *A la recherche du temps perdu.*

It is disconcerting that Harmony should diminish, and disconcerting to read at the end of *Histoire Extraordinaire* a note saying:

Certains estimeront peut-être que, désirant parler de Baudelaire, je n'ai réussi à parler que de moi-même. Il vaudrait mieux dire que c'est Baudelaire qui parlait de moi. Il parle de vous.[9] (*Ed. G.*)

But this does not prophesy misery and death for us all. Baudelaire the dandy stood in revolt against the complacent bourgeoisie of his time, as represented by General Aupick, supported by the anti-Americanism of Poe. Likewise Rabelais, Montaigne, Fourier, and Proust criticized their society and searched for a better one, drawing knowledge from wherever they could, from the past, from other authors, from within themselves, but all pushing into the future by their efforts to find something better than their state in the present and to express it in a way that would encourage others to join them in their dissatisfaction and their search.

The authors Butor has chosen to study, both in the volumes of *Répertoire*, his literary museums, and in the books he has produced to continue books which were in their turn based on earlier books, share his beliefs and widen our perspectives. His books and those of other authors, the real books and the imaginary ones they enfold, are interconnected and juxtaposed like the articles in the section of *L'Arc* No. 39 (which opens, we notice, with a passage from Fourier). The suggestions offered for study by *L'Arc* plunge for the most part into the past-personal (childhood) or social but the imaginary books we are to write are based in *The Thousand and One Nights*. Here lies one of many references to the stories which can be found throughout Butor's writings, one which should be pursued into the realm of the real as well as the imaginary, for its importance as a guide to Butor's reader cannot be over-estimated.

We remember that Scheherazade tells her tales in order to save her life, in order to create such an interest for the Sultan that he will keep her alive one more day. These are tales which must be compelling, which must provoke active curiosity and also beguile the listener into dream. Indeed we have seen that Butor tries to create a similar response. In conversation with Georges Charbonnier he compares the writer's situation to that of Scheherazade who is so utterly dependent upon the reaction of her audience for the prolongation of her very existence. Butor writes:

Eh bien: Tout écrivain est Schéhérézade, tout écrivain a en lui une menace de mort ... je dis bien, je dis "en lui", en lui et autour de lui. Cette menace qui est autour de lui le ronge, en quelque sorte, intérieurement. C'est contre cette épée de Damoclès, que l'écrivain parle. L'écrivain, en parlant, va lever indéfiniment la menace de mort qui pèse sur lui-même, et, naturellement, pèse aussi sur le développement de la société.[10]   (Ed. G.)

Thus the writer has a social role and a role of saviour similar to that of Scheherazade, saviour of the Sultan's people and critic, through her stories, of the state of the realm. The role of social critic is certainly one Butor accepts for we find, to mention but a sample, the condition of the Roman Catholic church, the educational system, the position of the Indians and coloured people in the USA. How though is the writer to save his people? Scheherazade accomplishes it by means of her story-telling ability; whether Butor will do likewise we shall perhaps find out if we look at his ways of using *The Thousand and One Nights*.

Butor reads to give a response to the writer, then writes to get a response from the reader; hence writing is for him a collaboration, but collaboration of many different kinds: between reader and author, author and his language, author and his culture. And in this sense *The Thousand and One Nights* is the product of such a series of collaborations between story-teller, listener, scribe and translator working across the centuries to give us the book which "a nourri la littérature européenne pendant deux siècles."[11] The tales have layer upon layer of interwoven significance, and to produce a similar effect, as we have seen, Butor constantly uses texts drawn from other authors' work as integral parts of his own creation. In each case the older text brings its own meanings into a new context and gains added significance thereby, meanwhile enriching the new work, so that together they provide reverberations which neither could have achieved alone. Each new combination creates a clash of outlook intended to provoke in the reader a perturbation similar to that produced by *The Thousand and One Nights* in the orderly world of

111

classical literature. The reader finds himself obliged to read the new work in a way to which he is not accustomed, and, his habits broken by the disorientation thus produced, his faculties are sharpened so that he becomes acutely aware of the things around him in relation to those which caused the disturbance. Suddenly another level of richness and complexity is added to his life.

Michel Butor's work is a constant grappling with the complexity of the world in which he finds himself. Just as the stories of *The Thousand and One Nights* emerge from one another like a set of Chinese boxes, and just as each becomes infinitely poorer and narrower in scope when removed from its context within the collection as a whole, so Butor's books, interesting as they may be individually, gain infinite breadth when considered as parts of a larger scheme. And in both cases the scheme is so mobile that the reader can choose his own paths within the work as a whole.[12] Butor has said that each book produces a problem which he attempts to solve in some way in a subsequent work; certainly links of this sort can be traced from book to book and the germ of each can be found in *Passage de Milan*.

Fiction makes society aware of itself in general, and in particular fills gaps in the information the individual has gleaned from his experience, presenting new examples in such a way that he can deal with situations of a similar kind should he ever need to do so. Butor explains the role of the novelist thus:

De même le romancier travaillant sur les éléments imaginaires, va pouvoir choisir ces éléments de telle sorte qu'il puisse aboutir à un texte dont la forme va être éclairante; cet exemple simplifié permettra ensuite d'étudier la réalité peu à peu dans toute sa complexité.[13]

In accordance with this belief, each of Butor's books, like each story in *The Thousand and One Nights*, formulates an interrelated series of problems in such a way that the reader recognizes them and can understand how they are treated. He is then set one for himself as it were, for just as Scheherazade interrupts her narration when the hero's predicament is at its worst, leaving the Sultan (and the reader) to imagine for himself the way he will escape some fearful end, and also, if he will, make a connection between the hero's position and that of the narrator of the tale, so Butor leaves his reader to complete for himself the work he has just read.

The culmination for the present is in *Les Sept Femmes de Gilbert le Mauvais*. Proust watches and transforms the world around him with a similar skill and purpose to that of Scheherazade who is an important point of reference within the work. Butor describes how Marcel has seven rooms: Combray, Paris I, Doncières, Balbec, Paris II, Venice and Tansonville. To each of the first six is connected a mother figure for whose death Marcel is responsible in some way: Mother, Gilberte, Saint-Loup, Grandmother, the Duchess of Guermantes and Albertine, and to each of these people is attached a section of society. The narrator must find a woman he cannot kill (thus he will find a society in which he can live) and she will help him bring the others back to life just as Scheherazade saves the Sultan's people from destruction and the princess fights the genie to save the monkey-prince. Butor writes:

La septième, la fidèle, celle qui méritera et établira l'adoration perpétuelle, ne pourra être que Schéhérézade, la conteuse, l'oeuvre salvatrice, la mère indestructible dans laquelle il pourra enfin renaître, être Marcel oui, si l'on veut, mais un autre Marcel, non plus Proust, et qui pourrait s'appeler René.

Et je vivrais dans l'anxiété de ne pas savoir si le Maître de ma destinée . . .
            (son propre corps),
moins indulgent que le sultan Sherier
            (lui-même enchanté),
le matin quand j'interromprais mon récit, voudrait bien surseoir à mon arrêt de mort
            (celui de l'oeuvre)
et me permettrait de reprendre la suite le prochain soir.
C'est que Schéhérézade ne peut sauver ses soeurs que dans la mesure où elle a subi elle aussi l'épreuve de la mort, où elle s'y offre chaque nuit, la risque. Ces mémoires des mille et une nuits doivent être des mémoires d'outretombe. Il faut qu'il y ait mort et résurrection non seulement du narrateur mais de la littérateur elle-même.[14]

By linking Scheherazade's salvation with that of Marcel at Tansonville, Butor reaffirms the statement that art provides the only way to an understanding and acceptance of the world, the only way its complexity can be transmitted in a form which is coherent and able to stimulate the imagination of others. Hence taking Proust as an authority, as indeed he has taken others throughout his career, he shows his belief in the power of literature as a social force, creating awareness, providing information, linking man wih his surroundings while giving significance to each, and also as an influence on the individual, stimulating him to thought, imagination and creativity. And Butor also demands that his reader should treat books as he does, letting them grow as they will:

What will happen to Louis Lécuyer in Egypt?
— Whatever you imagine, or see Jacques Revel abroad.
How can Revel solve the time problem?
— Your answer, or see La Modification.
What did Delmont write?
— La Modification, your novel, or what Vernier wrote for his nephew.

Here we have suggestions for imaginary works such as those listed in L'Arc, and beginning with "Le livre blanc mortel des Mille et Une Nuits".

Throughout his work Butor has tried to oblige his reader to read actively as his world gets richer and his problems more complex. Finally in Les Sept Femmes de Gilbert le Mauvais he pokes fun at those who refuse to look at the world with his breadth of vision, his flexibility (while still stretching the imagination and analytical faculties of the willing:

Les vrais professeurs à titres et à thèses prendront ce qu'ils pourront de mes divagations prismatiques, ajoutant au bas de leurs pages les paquets de notes de rigueur
  (pour faire passer aux yeux de certains ce que je dis, de quelle masse de jargon ne faudrait-il pas l'enrober) ;
  afin de borner ici la prolifération de ce capriccio critique, amusons-nous à leur proposer un concours.[15]

... [explanation of contest] ...

Le jeu consiste à retrouver la correspondance primitive entre les personnages de Combray et les allégories de Giotto ... Au chercheur alors qui se montrera comme ayant le mieux approché les données proustiennes, j'aurai le plaisir d'offrir une madeleine.[16]

The new problem is posed, and also the prize — the sensitivity of one who can extract the myths of his society and express them in a way that transmits the fullness of their possible significance to others. By reading properly, by looking at the world with such clarity and intuition, you may also become a Scheherazade or a Michel Butor searching for the philosopher's stone of protection against death, in your turn.

Just as Butor's concept of a spectacle relates to that of a site, so his concept of a book echoes that of a museum. The museum contains the art and artefacts created by individuals in the past grouped now with didactic intent; the book is Butor's creation in the present, his arrangement of elements personally selected for the purpose of generating understanding and thrust. Again we see that Butor turns us in upon his work and out into our own lives simultaneously, again he confronts reality with imagination for the greater illumination of each. Our initiation into comprehension and expression is almost complete.

CHAPTER VI: FOOTNOTES

[1] See also L. Dällenbach: "Le livre et ses miroirs dans l'oeuvre romanesque de Michel Butor," *Archives des Lettres Modernes*, No. 135 (Paris 1972).

[2] "Le roman comme recherche," *Répertoire*, p. 9: "... it is evident that the form being a principle of choice ... new forms will reveal new things in reality, new links and, naturally, the more their internal coherence is affirmed in respect to the other forms the more rigorous they will be."

[3] "Le roman comme recherche," p. 9: "The search for new novel forms with greater power of integration therefore plays a triple role with reference to the consciousness we have of the real, of denunciation, exploration and adaptation. The novelist who refuses to do this work, who does not upset habits, nor demand of his readers any special effort, who does not force him to turn back upon himself, to question positions taken up a long time ago, has an easier success, certainly, but he becomes the accomplice of this deep malaise, this night in which we are all struggling. He makes the reflexes of consciousness still more inflexible, makes its awakening more difficult, he contributes to its stifling so that even if he has generous intentions his work is, in the final analysis, a poison."

[4] "Intervention à Royaumont," p. 272: "I do not write novels in order to sell them but to obtain a unity in my life; writing is a spinal column for me: and to quote Henry James' phrase 'A novelist is someone for whom nothing is lost'. At present there is no other literary form with as great a power as the novel. Within it feelings or reason can be used to join in an extremely precise way what seem to be the most insignificant incidents of daily life to thoughts, intuitions and dreams which seem far removed from day to day language. Thus it is a splendid way to hold oneself upright, to continue to live intelligently inside a quasi-furious world which assails one from all sides."

[5] "Our world has just discovered another (and who can say whether it is the last of its brothers ...)."

[6] Act V, sc. viii: "And without having died she is dead for him."

[7] "Something for nothing, Tell me who you are haunting."

[8] "You will be judged by your culture."

[9] P. 267: "Some people will think perhaps that while wanting to talk about Baudelaire, I have only managed to talk about myself. It would be better to say that it was Baudelaire who spoke about me. He talks about you." See also J. Kolbert, "Points of view in Michel Butor's criticism: Geometry and Optics," *Kentucky Romance Quarterly*, XVIII, 2 (1971).

[10] G. Charbonnier, *Entretiens avec Michel Butor*, pp. 41-42: "Every author is Scheherazade, every author has the threat of death within him. ... I repeat 'within him' within him and around him. This threat which is all around him gnaws at him, so to speak, from the inside. The writer speaks against this sword of Damocles. By speaking the author lifts indefinitely the threat of death which weighs on him and which naturally weighs on all social development too."

[11] *Ibid.*, p. 41: "has nourished European literature for two centuries."

[12] "Les tendances du roman français après la dernière guerre," *NM* (*Neusprachliche Mitteilungen aus Wissenschaft und Praxis*), 41 (1966), p. 206.

[13] *Ibid.*, p. 201: "In the same way the novelist, working on imaginary elements will be able to choose these elements in such a way that he can arrive at a text that is enlightening; this simplified example will permit him to study reality afterwards bit by bit in all its complexity."

[14] *Les Sept Femmes de Gilbert le Mauvais*, pp. 46-47: "The seventh, the faithful one who will deserve and will establish perpetual adoration can only be Scheherazade the storyteller, the saving work, the indestructible mother in whom he can at last be reborn, be Marcel yes, if you wish, but another Marcel, no longer Proust, and who could be called René. *And I should live in the anxiety of not knowing whether the Master of my destiny* . . . (his own body) *less indulgent than the Sultan Sheriar* (himself enchanted) *in the morning when I interrupt my tale would reprieve my death sentence* (that of the work) *and would allow me to continue it the next evening.* The fact is that Scheherazade can only save her sisters to the extent that she herself has undergone the test of death of which she takes the risk every night. These memories of the thousand and one nights should be memories from beyond the grave. There must be death and resurrection not only of the narrator, but of literature itself."

[15] *Ibid.*, p. 83: "Real professors, those with degrees and theses, will take what they can from my prismatic wanderings, and add at the bottom of their pages the bundles of compulsory footnotes (in what a mass of jargon would what I say have to be enveloped in order to be accepted by certain people); to cut short the proliferation of this critical capriccio here, let us amuse ourselves by offering them a competition."

[16] *Ibid.*, p. 89: "The game consists in finding the original correspondance between the characters at Combray and Giotto's allegories. . . . To the researcher who proves to have come nearest to the Proustian data I shall have the pleasure of offering a madeleine."

CHAPTER VII

Symbolic Reflections

Michel Butor's work is concerned with one major problem from which all others spring: the problem of man's position in the modern world. The author's way of treating this joins his work to the age-old tradition of quest literature. Like Lancelot and Parcifal he is searching for a grail, like an alchemist for a philosopher's stone, like the heroes of *The Thousand and One Nights* for some hidden treasure, and as in the Grail legends, the alchemist's experiments and the princes' journeying, the quest is in many ways more important than its result, for from it wisdom is gained.

For Butor the quest has three aspects, social, personal and professional, all of which we have looked at earlier. The search to understand the situation of any given society can be found in the exploration of its various sites. The movement between the sites chosen by Butor offers possibilities for the development of the whole of Western Europe:

France — Europe — Egypt — the Orient — USA (New Mexico)
/
USA (east)

A direct shift from Europe to the USA is not satisfactory. What is needed is an understanding of other forces which have been influential in the world in order to arrive at a wider comprehension, a more basic grasp of the universal pattern. Travelling brings one sort of knowledge — that of the outside world in time — a social awareness.

The second quest is a personal one which was discussed at the beginning of this study in connection with the presentation of characters. We saw that Butor began with fragmented, juxtaposed characters whose facets gradually joined to form a single unified personality, fictional at first and then that of the author himself, who, once prepared to speak in his own voice, finds himself able to include his family in his work also. (His wife appears in *Où*, his wife and daughters in "Blues des projets", *Travaux d'approche*, and in

117

Matière de Rêves). This development is inevitably closely linked with the previous one and also with Butor's critical work, for in his studies of other authors he (and his reader) must recognize his own situation.

In his writings he encourages his readers to begin similar quests for themselves. Each of his fictional works has an elaborate system for forcing the reader into activity; these systems range from the literary references in *Degrés* to the vote in *Votre Faust* and the provocative non-section at the end of *Portrait de l'artiste en jeune singe*. Finally comes the open challenge in *Les Sept Femmes de Gilbert le Mauvais*, a work which, like all the criticism, shows the reader how best to profit from the books at his disposition.

The formulation of constantly evolving and interrogative forms and the study of such forms in other people produce the third quest, that of adequate literary expression as a vehicle for his ideas and aims. He is searching to understand his world for himself. He needs to express what he learns and to express it in such a way that his reader begins to question his own situation.[1] As Butor is advancing all the time he cannot offer solutions to the problems he poses even if he wished to do so. Instead he offers a method by which to grasp the most important elements of the present situation and recognize the ever-changing patterns these are forming all the time. His writing is a constant struggle to create a system by which to understand the systems around him quickly enough to be able to use his knowledge within that system before it is transformed.

Butor's method has two distinct elements which merge as success is neared, the "factual" part drawn from history and geography, from direct observation and learning, and the "symbolic" part which transforms rational knowledge through imagination and dream. We have seen Butor explore a place (Niagara Falls for example) and examine its makeup in detail until he is able to extract its essence: the myth of the site. In this case Niagara reveals the cycle of death and rebirth which every hero undergoes before achieving true wisdom (we think of Scheherazade and the position of the author) and which passes unrecognized by the visitors who have ceased to know the reason for their pilgrimage.

Butor shows his reader how to examine a site right at the beginning of his career, in *L'Emploi du Temps*, and returns to it time and again, most recently in *Rabelais* when he refers to the significance of everything found in the Abbey of Thélème. Having understood the significance of the environment, each person must teach what he knows to the succeeding generations. We are offered two forms this instruction might take in the description of the cosmic dance of the Zuni Indians in *Où* and in Fourier's projection of a universal system as illustrated in *La Rose des Vents*. In both cases music is an important element of the presentation, imposing a flexible but defined form on the patterns of inter-relationships proposed.

Fourier is a prime representative of the role of the imagination in understanding, which Butor has already stressed in the dream sequences of *Portrait de l'artiste en jeune singe*. In the dreams, events of the daily life of the young Butor are linked to what he has read, and the whole is metamorphosed into an image of much wider import. The very choice of the alchemical system on which Butor draws in the book gives a sense of multi-level quest, of the power of symbol and the importance of close analysis of any given text. If we examine the hermetic elements in *Portrait* more closely we shall find that a key is provided for many references throughout the author's work.

Portrait de l'artiste en jeune singe contains within itself its keys, secrets and multiple possibilities. The most important key is to be found in the title. Direct homage to Joyce's fictional autobiography and to that of Dylan Thomas covers more esoteric allusion. Joyce belonged to the Rosicrucian movement which surrounded W. B. Yeats at the beginning of the twentieth century, and his works contain so many levels of language, literary reference, ritual and mythology that it is impossible to grasp them all. It is this protean aspect which attracts Butor and about which he writes in the essays on Joyce in *Répertoire* and *Répertoire II*. His reading of *Finnegans Wake* indicates the way in which his own work should be approached. Each line, paragraph or page should be read and reread in a way that allows all the elements in it to combine and recombine in constantly evocative patterns. Joyce plays with language; Butor juxtaposes works of art, historical eras and objects to attain the same end.

His primary symbol is the monkey. A reader who considers its literary implications only will think that Butor is mocking himself and the way he apes Joyce and Thomas, but the second section of *Portrait* bears the heading:

En Egypte, le dieu de l'écriture, Thot, était souvent représenté par un singe.[2] (*Ed. G.*)

As Thoth is also Hermes Trismagisthus, the god of alchemy, and as

119

the alchemists used the symbol of the monkey, the very title of *Portrait* unites and presents simultaneously both aspects of the symbolic structure, the duality in the nature of the work and the hermetic language in which it is to be written. It is a major key to the whole.

The alchemists thought that man was the ape of God and that the alchemical process was an attempt to understand the Creation of the world by reproducing its chemical development on a smaller scale. Similarly Butor uses the symbols and procedures of the hermetic art to explain his personal growth. Since Egypt is the fatherland of alchemy, all allusions to Egypt are vested immediately with a power much superior to their mere autobiographical relevance to Butor. The section of *Portrait* entitled "Voyage" is under the protection of Thoth. Herein lies the reason for the choice of the tale of the Second Calender: the prince is turned into a monkey. The "Envoi", "L'Autre Voyage", shows the direction the next mental and physical journeys of the author will take. How could he not leave for Egypt? The decision has been foretold in the "Préface" where he says:

C'était avant mon départ pour l'Egypte, c'est-à-dire que pour moi cela remonte très loin, car l'Egypte m'a été comme une seconde terre natale, j'y ai vécu pour ainsi dire une seconde enfance.[3] (*Ed. G.*)

And suddenly the statement becomes abundantly clear; this second childhood is the product of the alchemical quest and is the rebirth of the adept.

The discovery of alchemy, initiation into its teaching and the resulting personal development are stages in the author's life which produce the natural divisions in the book. *Portrait* is divided into three parts, each of which has two titles printed in different types: those in roman letters (Prélude, Voyage, Envoi) explain the structure of the book and what it offers to the reader. Those in capitals (LE DOCTEUR H, LE SAINT-EMPIRE, L'AUTRE VOYAGE) indicate the theme which is essential to the comprehension of the section. The sections describe the author's past, present and future.

Inside this triple division are others whose titles are used for their evocative power. The "Prélude" is divided into five chapters, the "Voyage" into fifteen and the "Envoi" is a blank that the future should fill. It has a title, but nothing else and hence confronts the reader as a unity, a void pregnant with possibility. There are three sections, five and fifteen chapters. The number of sections and chapters is not a matter of chance. These numbers are important in numerology and kabbalistic studies. The theory on which the scientific discoveries of Jabir, alchemist at the court of Haroun-al-Raschid, were based was created by means of a square of primary numbers. Five was in the centre and the other figures were arranged in such a way that the sum of every line was fifteen. Fifteen thus became a natural number which consequently played a part in all combinations and movements of the natural elements.

The three dominates all alchemical experiments, representing in the Christian era the Holy Trinity in various guises. Of these the most important are the sun, moon and mercury; the white and red stone and the elixir, body, soul and spirit. In addition the geometrical symbol for life in primary matter is $\lozenge$. The first triangle $\triangledown$ represents water from which everything was made. The other $\triangle$ is fire, the traditional manifestation of the holy spirit. Fulcanelli explains the concept in *Les Demeures Philosophales*,[4] a book which plays a major role in *Portrait* and stresses the inter-relation of the alchemical quest and Christian aspiration.

All symbolic objects are grouped in threes in the fifteen chapters of "Voyage", and frequently a single example of the same thing, French instead of German, will be found as a guide in the "Prélude". There are three German castles where Butor studies alchemy, but his initial interest was created in a French one. He has to learn three foreign languages, Latin, Old High German, and modern German, but he first reads the subject in French. In castle H he finds the work of three German alchemists, Basilus Valentinus, Jacob Boehme and Athanasius Kircher, but he has previously discovered that of the Frenchman Nicholas Flamel. He meets Dr. H[5] in France and he is the Hungarian who interests Butor in the Holy Roman Empire with its threefold geographical division into Germany, Austria and Hungary, as well as arranging the young man's stay in Germany.

Among the authors whose books are quoted in *Portrait*, the alchemists are German, Franz Werfel and Alfred Kubin, the science-fiction, fantasy writers are Austrian and Jules Verne sets his tale in Hungary. Hungary is central to the historical and symbolic development, the point of contact with the Middle Eastern triplicity of Egypt, the Ottoman Empire (Jabir and Haroun-al-Raschid) and Palestine. These are represented by *Joseph in Egypt* and *The Thousand and One Nights*. The books quoted can also be classified according to period: Mediaeval-Renaissance, eighteenth century and modern. The visual arts are also threefold; engraving, painting and sculpture. To make this grouping even more obvious three kinds of type are used for the chapter headings; roman type indicates life in France, gothic script shows life in Germany and copperplate for dreams.

The actual printing of the book, chapter headings aside, is done with two typefaces. Roman letters are used when Butor's daily life is the subject, but when he describes his state of mind in dream form then italics are used instead. (All references to Egypt are in italics too.) The visual distinction is a constant reminder of the alchemical paradox, the continual struggle to try and unite theory, practice and spiritual exercise. Just as Hungary links east to west, so Dr. H shows Butor the way to past and future, to alchemy and science-fiction. Did this man form the ideas on science-fiction that Butor expresses in *Répertoire* and *Passage de Milan?* Is he the prototype of Samuel Léonard?[6] Be this as it may, the division between life and fantasy in "Voyage" is indicative of the struggle between elements which are finally combined in perfect form, and also of the philosophical-practical split which produces the problems of Faust, and the eventual weakening and quasi-disappearance of alchemy. Thus all alchemy has two aspects. What Butor offers his reader has two sides too. Reality is in opposition to dream, the secular to the religious; there is always a choice of interpretation.

After three the number most important to the structure of *Portrait* is seven — the number of days of the week of the Creation. Butor quotes from the description given by Jacob Boehme in his *Mysterium Magnum*. Each of the odd-numbered chapters of "Voyage" mentions one day. Butor stays seven weeks in the castle, he dreams seven dreams, the Count teaches him seven ways of playing patience. There are seven stages in the initiation of an alchemist, seven chemical reactions during the transmutation of lead to gold, seven planets as symbols of the primary elements of the natural world. Boehme lists them all.

Seven has always been a magic number, but in *Portrait de l'artiste en jeune singe* (a seven word title) it stands for the infinite possibility present at the end of Creation week. The German chapters each describe one day of the week, but of a different week, hence Butor has to leave on a Monday because the seven weeks of his stay passed concurrently with the seven days described. A double time-scheme is produced which incorporates the unique into the universal, personal into general, in such a way that an ordinary person can take his place in the cosmos, as the quotations from Boehme's explanation of the Creation constantly indicate.

Nothing in the structure of *Portrait* is gratuitous. Man's position in the universe is like that of a day within time and eternity. A single personal life is drawn into civilization as a whole as Butor describes his past and his stay. At the same time his seven dreams suggest both that which is beyond man's understanding, and also the split between the public and private aspects of any personality. The dreams have a hallucinatory surrealism; daily happenings, books read, looked at or remembered, objects which have attracted attention, all pour into the dreamer's mind. But every reference is familiar to the reader, so that the kaleidoscopic presentation provokes a freshness of thought and re-evaluation of fixed ideas, the results of which are created by unexpected subconscious association. It is a deliberate use of fantasy responses.

In direct contrast the daily happenings are described in a way which is designed to prevent the pursuit of a line of thought to its end. Logical progress is interrupted by sensory distraction. The simultaneity of perception is recreated in such a fashion that it is impossible to escape into traditional, linear reading habits. *Portrait* is experienced not read. Butor builds the vastness of the universe around each reader who should then adapt the Butorian world to suit his own character. This will in turn be changed a little by the very exercise of adaptation. By his use of the capriccio technique Butor is able to show at one and the same time a schema of the world and human reaction to its complexity. He demands of his reader experience, understanding and flexibility, and yet has the skill to retain an atmosphere of intellectual amusement.

Like a game Butor's work contains its own key to rules and meaning. He quotes from the "Préface au lecteur" of the first alchemical treatise he read, the passage where the editor explains the author's way of disguising what he has to say "par une artificieuse méthode" so that the unworthy should not misuse it. Similarly, any reader who is prepared to make an effort will understand Butor and appreciate the form of his work. Hence from a study of the number seven he will be led inevitably to a closer study of the seven dream chapters, whose titles follow, in allegorical form, the seven stages of transmutation, and thence to the chapters of reality.

Butor leaves France with a closed book entrusted to him by Dr. H, his guide and mentor. It is *Les Demeures Philosophales* in which Fulcanelli explains the symbolic system of alchemy and the way the adepts incorporated them into the very construction of their houses. The closed book is "the Book of the Apocalypse, its pages held by seven seals, the book of initiation which is offered by those who are bound to teach the highest truths" (Vol. I, p. 312). The perusal of Fulcanelli's book reveals new dimensions in Butor's symbols and an insight into the way he uses them. The "Voyage" is seen to be the long and careful preparation of the primary matter, hidden under an allegory of the pilgrimage of St. James of Compostella. This image links the initiate to his work for the first time, because the term traveller or pilgrim is used with equal frequency to refer either to the alchemist or to mercury. Once the journey has been accomplished the transmutation experiments can begin. Here they are listed in order:

1. L'aller (setting out)
2. *L'homme de grande vieillesse* (the very old man)
3. La bibliothèque (the library)
4. *L'étudiante* (the girl student)
5. Minérologie (minerology)
6. *Le forestier* (the forester)
7. Le chemin de ronde (the battlements)
8. *La métamorphose* (metamorphosis)
9. Mundus Subterraneus
10. *Les patiences* (the patience games)
11. Orbites (orbits)
12. *Le tournoi* (the tournament)
13. Le Musée Allemand (the German museum)
14. *Le bannissement* (banishment)
15. L'adieu (the farewell)

Italics indicate dream, roman type reality. The titles give an immediate impression of superficial understanding; the various parts of the castle, the dream people, are easily recognizable, but on reflection the relationship between titles becomes much more complicated and there emerges a symbolic progression on two levels, each of which holds the key to the other. The even chapters are in the allegorical language of alchemy, the odd ones contain Butor's autobiographical symbols and they are inseparable.

Thus after "L'aller" of Chapter I comes *"L'homme de grande vieillesse"*. He represents Saturn who ate his own children so that they could be reborn. Butor quotes the description given by Basilus Valentinus (*Portrait*, p. 33). He is the lead which fixes mercury by cutting off its feet with his scythe, the philosopher's stone and the father of all metals (Fulcanelli, Vol. I, p. 166). *"L'étudiante"* is mercury which is often disguised as a virgin. Here then are the stable and volatile elements essential to alchemy and which can be transposed easily into analogies of reality and fantasy. Indeed the transposition is indicated by the titles "La bibliothèque" and "Minérologie"; human reason acts on the primary matter of the material universe. The mineral collection in Castle H has as important a role in *Portrait* as that of the library.

"*Le forestier*" is easily recognizable as the woodsman, the man with the staff of the *Demeures Philosophales*. Fulcanelli explains it thus:

The lopped branch held by this artisan seems to indicate the measure of his industry. Yet however, it is indeed our withered tree. . . . The *Withered Tree* was a souvenir of Palestine; it was the tree that grew near Hebros, that had flourished since the Creation but lost its leaves the day Christ was crucified, and withered away from that time. . . . It was adopted by the philosophers to express the inertia of metal, that is, the state human industry gives to metal by melting it. Hermetic esoterism teaches that metallic bodies remain alive and have a vegetable power as long as they are in the form of ore. They are in contact with the specific agent or mineral spirit which assures their vitality, nutrition and evolution for the natural term at the end of which they take on the aspect of properties of true silver or gold. Once this has been achieved the agent leaves the body which ceases to live, is fixed and no longer susceptible to change. (Vol. I, pp. 186-188)

Hence "*Le forestier*" protects the early stages of experimentation much as the "chemin de ronde" forms the first and outer defence of Castle H — a role analogous to that of the rockbed of the mineral, because once the castle has been deserted by the spirit it was built to protect its form will evolve no more.

"*La métamorphose*" is what happens to the spirit of the metal when it is recovered from its bed. Alchemy is based on successive metamorphoses by which the raw material is transformed into a precious form approaching perfection. Butor refers to this transformation when he speaks of a "grotto of intellectual treasure, discussions which should be written on purple sheets . . . " (*Portrait*, p. 39). And from this idea of a cave arises the title "Mundus Subterraneus". This bears a threefold reference: to the "grottes" of Pommersfelden castle which contain the whole of hermetic philosophy (the mineral world, the four elements and the seasons); secondly to the use of Latin (which refers back to Chapter 6 of the "Prélude": "Turba philosophorum"), indicating a change which is difficult to understand and thus appears to be hidden more completely than the others; thirdly, it is the title of one of the works by Athanasius Kircher.

"Les patiences" are games which contain their own solution. The player must know the rules and have enough patience to play over and over again until he succeeds in completing the pattern. This title clearly indicates the method to be followed when reading *"La méta-morphose"* — the reader must repeat all the steps leading to success as many times as necessary to achieve that aim. The Count teaches Butor seven games. He begins with *L'Almanach de Gotha* and *Les Moyens de parvenir,* schemas for material success, and at the end of the stay (Butor's period of initiation) he shows him *La Roue des Planètes* which incorporates the entire universe. This last game explains the choice of the title "Orbites". The seven planets revolve in the sky according to cosmic rules; likewise they spin in the mind of the alchemist because in hermetic language they are allegories of the stages of experimentation.

"Le tournoi" takes up the theme of the implacable struggle between two sides, the primary elements, mineral and metal (the old man and the student), whose mutual destruction marks an important step in the alchemical process. The tournament or joust is a term and practice dating from the time when the influence of alchemy was at its height and so was that of the Holy Roman Empire. The parallel title "Le Musée Allemand" contains the same ideas and adds an autobiographical element to them by connecting to Butor's belief in the dynamic influence of the past.

"Le bannissement" implies a compulsory departure, the descent into the underworld which brings enlightenment. J. van Lennep in *Art et Alchimie*[7] compares the alchemist to the legendary hero who must overcome a series of obstacles before obtaining the marvel he is seeking, who must gain a full understanding of himself on his journey through the underworld and through death achieve birth. Hence he alone is capable of paradise because he alone has the full power with which man was endowed. "L'adieu" marks the necessary departure from Germany, for Butor's rebirth is to take place in Egypt, as foretold in the first lines of *Portrait.*

The book turns back on itself and now is the time to look at the titles of the "Prélude". Just as "LE SAINT-EMPIRE" combines the spiritual with the material and at the same time indicates the historical period which is most important in the second section, so "LE DOCTEUR H" is the tutelary of the first. He symbolizes both guide and initiate, the one who incites the disciple to begin his studies.

126

From him comes "L'invitation" to set out for Germany. Working backwards from "L'invitation" the next heading introduces the term "Turba philosophorum". This is a weapon familiar to alchemists and is the title of a seventeenth-century Germany treatise, indicating the state of mind of the initiate. The "Journées de lecture" are clearly the young Butor's preparation for his future studies. "Hongrois" is Dr. H's nationality and also that of the very old man (lead and sulphur) in Basilus Valentinus' book (*Portrait*, p. 34). The doctor is linked closely with his work; Hungary is vampire country according to Jules Verne, and in hermetic terminology "vampire" refers to the universal dissolvant, the great Alkaest which extracts from any metal the sulphur which is its lifeblood — hence the analogy.

Through the chapter headings the alchemical process has been disclosed. Just as colours are important to show the chemical permutations obtained by the alchemist, so they are important in the dream chapters of *Portrait* to indicate changing relationships. The key to this is given in the first chapter when Butor writes of the difficulty he has in seeing the colour of the eyes of anyone he knows well. A person's soul can be read in his eyes as the secrets of the universe can be seen in the athanor. The eye is as difficult to look at as the sun, and the sun, like the gold the alchemists seek, is a symbol of divine perfection. Hence colours are used in an ascending order from black to gold and indicate certain stages of development.

Immediately following this enigmatic chapter comes the reader's introduction to the author's guide and mentor, Dr. H. He encourages Butor's leaning towards hermeticism and helps in his education. By the use of quotation in *Portrait* tremendously evocative power is drawn from the fact that the doctor is Hungarian. We have seen that Hungary links Islam at the height of its science to Mediaeval Europe, and above all it bears traces of the Huns. Huns, Hungary and Dr. H play an important role in *Portrait*, and thus must be linked to Fulcanelli's long discussion of the importance of the letter H (Vol. II, pp. 144-145) in the book Butor carries to Castle H for his tutor. H was chosen by philosophers as the symbol of the universal spirit of all things, the active principle of nature (hence the shape of many cathedral façades). It is the *seventh* letter of the Greek alphabet and the first of the word for the sun, source of power and light. Likewise it is at the heart of the *three* letter monogram of Christ (IHS), and yet it is the symbol of man: Iesus *Hominum* Salvator. *Portrait* is born under a powerful sign.

127

Within the book Butor creates a world in which every detail has a second meaning, where diverse aspects of the same problem are linked in many ways. Although it is not possible to exhaust the possibilities of a work which is so evocative and so complex, the principal symbols may be isolated and considered in some detail. First the characters: they are real people, but after Fulcanelli's interpretation of the woodsman who turns into the Butorian "forestier" it is interesting to note the number of princes and their employees who wear forester's dress. In the Second Calender's Tale of *The Thousand and One Nights*, the profession of woodcutter is the prince's point of departure.

Count W,[8] Butor's host at H, often wears forester's dress. He is lame when the Frenchman arrives and his physical limitations, which are clearly visible, represent his linguistic condition, which in turn is a symbol of his understanding. As his French improves so does his infirmity. The lame Count in his castle evokes the Fisher King of the Grail legend. He needs the young man's help to recapture the ability he has lost and in his turn initiates the visitor into the secret knowledge he holds (patience games). We remember that this is only possible if the young man asks the right questions. When he does the king is restored to power and the initiate goes on to achieve more perfect understanding elsewhere.

Language is here again the symbol of comprehension. French is the language of the first alchemical treatise mentioned and of the one Butor takes to Germany. It follows that a good grasp of it is the sign of a mind ready to begin its initiation. A knowledge of man's means of communication is, of course, essential to an understanding of his thought. Butor establishes a scale of hermeticism which indicates the degree of attainment. The age of the language and the complexity of its alphabet increase together with the relative difficulty of the ideas expressed. This is clear to every reader whether or not he is able to understand the quotations Butor uses or read the books mentioned. Of course if he can do this he will have a firmer grasp on *Portrait* and everything it stands for.

All information is taken from ancient texts; it is an age-old wisdom passed down from reader to reader amongst an elite. Those who are born into this group meet by choice and the masters guide and encourage lay-brothers whom they have invited into their circle. Retirement from the modern world is essential to the success of the study; the group of philosophers meet outside Paris, Butor is exiled in the castle. The old castles were centres of culture, government

128

and religion so the libraries are to be found within their walls. Castle H was not only the seat of the prince but of the priest, for it enclosed the only church in Harburg. The prince of Pommersfelden was both prince and archbishop of the region. Hence the castles are symbols of the totality of a historical period.

Castle H is perched on a cliff dominating the town of Harburg. It was built by the very society that built the town and is in the same style, but its superior position is symbolic of the treasure it holds. Unlike Castel H, Pommersfelden castle stands in its own grounds aloof from town and world. The marvels it contains have no connection with the society around it. Does this imply that the knowledge Butor seeks was everywhere available during the Middle Ages but that by the seventeenth century it was the exclusive property of the ruling classes? Other comparisons he makes would suggest that this was so. To illustrate the theme of historical degeneration indicated by the castles Butor selects works of three engravers: Dürer's *Apocalypse* (late 15th century), Callot's *Miseries and Misfortunes of War* (17th century) and Hogarth's *Rake's Progress* (18th century). The books quoted may be classified in the same way. The modern authors (Kubin, Mann, Werfel) dream of societies which are geographically or chronologically distant from their own, preferring to escape actuality. The eighteenth-century authors have little weight: *Le Cavalier de Faublas* is very like the Rake, *Le Cabinet des Fées* provides an allegorical view of the world which uses alchemical elements in an inferior manner. It teaches a double morality: one for appearance's sake and one for daily use. And like *The Thousand and One Nights* from which it is largely derived, it indicates man's need to dream.

In his criticism[9] Butor expresses the opinion that fairy tales maintain a moral balance in the society to which they belong, but that new ones suitable to this age cannot be written. Instead it is the task of science-fiction to create the mythology of modern man. As early as 1953 in this essay on "La crise de croissance de la science-fiction" (*Répertoire*, pp. 186-194), he praises Jules Verne, Franz Werfel and H. P. Lovecraft for reintegrating the mystery of the unknown into daily life, and all three reappear in *Portrait*. The books Butor quotes are chosen to show the continuous need for fantasy and the unceasing quest for something beyond the degeneracy of the ordinary world.

The most important text in *Portrait* is *The Thousand and One Nights*, source of many of the most extravagant fantasies of European literature. Even without recognizing the tale of the Second Calender, in which the prince follows Butor's development stage by stage, the general influence in the dream chapters is quite obvious. It is significant that the book is found at the highest point in each library and that the Second Calender begins his tale on the *fiftieth* night. Butor spends seven weeks — forty-nine days — in Harburg, hence the tale could well be substituted into "L'Autre Voyage" of the "Envoi" to represent a supranormal development and the rich world which is now open to him.

The Thousand and One Nights is made up of a series of marvels and allegories which are inextricably intertwined. Within the whole work an apparently ficticious world is created which proves more real than the daily routine which surrounds it, for it alone has the power to protect the narrator from death. Consciousness of Scheherazade's fate is maintained by means of quotations from the notebook of the executioner of H.[10] Dream and literature maintain life. Reality is transformed into dream and by this metamorphosis salvation is achieved. Like the prince-monkey who saves his own life through his ability to write, Butor-artist-monkey is reconciled to the world by means of his creation which apes the creation of the universe. In this way every artist becomes an alchemist, every observer a disciple.

Butor becomes the pupil of the Count who as we mentioned before shows him how to play many varieties of patience. The games the Count teaches have a dual purpose: that of teaching perseverance and also that of drawing attention to the major themes of *Portrait*. Egypt, alchemy, and the initiation struggle against death give *Joseph en Egypte*, the *Château des Karpathes*, and the *Mille et Une Nuits*. The importance of origins and social criticism is indicated by the *Almanach de Gotha* and the *Moyens de Parvenir*; the attitude of the outside world towards the initiate gives *Chasse à la Sorcière*, and the cosmic aim of the work by *La Roue des planètes*. The games stress the need to read the books mentioned and in addition the rules of each one provide a summary of the book on which it is based. *Chasse à la Sorcière* provides as clear a warning of the danger of the quest as does the alarm bell in the library.

Each game has rules which must be understood if one is to succeed. Books should be analysed in the same way; hence a link is established between the library and the mineral collection in the castle. Neither is open to the casual tourist. The stones hide the marvels of the physical world from all but students of minerology; likewise for the alchemist the extraction of metals from their ore is the practical revelation of the spiritual quest. And every mineral is slowly turning to gold. Thus the proliferation of names of minerals in *Portrait* indicates the vast numbers of treasures always awaiting discovery.

Names are used to establish connections between people and things, though these prove evocative rather than informative, the resemblance being in the initials only. There is a Count W and a Castle W which is of minor interest in *Portrait*. Dr. H is linked to Castle H which thus becomes a "demeure philosophale". H is made up of two villages, one beside the river and the other around the castle. Budapest, the capital of Hungary, is a double city too. Dr. H is Hungarian and Butor is descended from the Huns on his mother's side. His very name has the meaning in Hungarian of "mobilier" and Butor soon learns to recognize the word in German. The idea of "mobilier" — that which is personal and movable — suggests both the treasures in the castle and the mobility of metamorphosis, the ever-changing colour of eyes and the shift of dreams. Transformation is the key to alchemy and the elixir sought is produced by the metamorphosis of a bottle of Hungarian wine. Tokaj has the appearance of liquid gold and being very intoxicating it provides the courage necessary to face the vampire of *The Thousand and One Nights*. (Similarly an intoxication caused by books sets off the library alarm.) Butor thinks he finds this wine in the count's home and for him it is a sign that he has learned all that H has to offer him.

The wine is a symbol of thirst and of ultimate success in its context (see below Rabelais' use of the same symbol), but the grouping of the symbols varies constantly. Most of them are optimistic, but a few suggest that the initiate's task is impossible. The portrait of Charlemagne as emperor and priest, master of things temporal and spiritual, is a copy. The witches, the executions and the story from *The Thousand and One Nights* create paradoxes which cannot be solved satisfactorily. Perhaps the capriccio's greatest value lies in the evocative power of its paradoxes.

The quotations from the alchemical works and *The Thousand and One Nights* are responsible for the effect of much of the book. They stimulate both the intellect and the imagination of the reader in such a way that he shares the author's experience and joins alchemists and philosophers in the search for his own interpretation of the structure of the universe. First the borrowings show how much an author owes to the civilization around him. Secondly they link by similarity or disparity of ideas the books which are juxtaposed in this way. The quotations provide an atmosphere which the author of the book which frames them could not have created by himself. *Portrait* is a work which is in code, a code which is immediately accessible to the reader who is prepared to spend a little time and effort to decipher it. The interplay of symbol and structure produces the multitude of possibilities which are the basis of *Portrait*'s force. "Extremely complex relationships can be constructed on very simple foundations" Butor wrote in "L'alchimie et son langage" in 1953, and fourteen years later his capriccio proves that this is indeed the case.

It is with reference to *Portrait* that we realize the importance of colour in the descriptions in *6 810 000 litre d'eau par seconde* which antedates *Portrait* and in *Où* which, coming after it, profits from the richness of resonance previously created.

The importance given to texts from other authors has been considered in some detail above, but the use of *The Thousand and One Nights* situates the influence of the stories firmly in the centre of Butor's world. The very name carries for us connotations of riches, sensuousness, danger, magic, narrow escapes from death — especially underground and at the hands of evil spirits — and final reward. Already we see that the pattern falls into that of the universal hero,[11] a pattern which Butor uses disguised as the passage through a cellar (*Passage de Milan*), a labyrinth (*L'Emploi du Temps*), tunnels (*La Modification*), the metro (*Degrés*), a trip under a waterfall (*6 810 000 litres*), "les grottes" the garden room at Pommersfelden (*Portrait*). Obviously in both worlds we are supposed to find significance in what is put before us.

At first the story of the Second Calender would seem to have been chosen to show the division between fantasy and reason, the dark mysteries of the East and the spiritual illumination of the West, but gradually it becomes clear that the colours of the athanor are the colours of the cave and that the prince is undergoing, in the flesh, the trials of the young Butor's mind and spirit. They become identified with one another as the significance of the daytime is extracted and turned into myth at night, presented no longer in arguments, but in brilliant images fitting the pattern of the hero. Only when both forms are compatible can understanding be reached.

Quite a number of parallels may be drawn between the tales and Butor's work. They share a similar sense of movement in life, of progress seen as a journey, of the problems of language and communication. Most of their heroes are lost in foreign lands and always they are learning to deal with new situations, acquiring knowledge and wisdom ready for the time when their trials will be over. As well as these themes and the frequent sensuousness of the description, the works share a joy in the intricate details of a world which expresses itself in a proliferation of colours, patterns and objects. The clearest example is that of the list of minerals in *Portrait* which conjures up pictures of grottos hung with marvels just like the one in the description of *La Grotte Merveilleuse* by Jules Verne which is quoted in *L'Arc* (p. 76). Samuel Léonard's apartment in *Passage de Milan* produces a similar Arabian Nights effect. Link these to the all-pervading taint of Egypt and to the descriptions of Marco Polo's China and the Orient meets the Western world again, this time not in France but in America, an America which struggles with France for possession of Butor, caught in a cosmic dance belonging to another all-embracing world view — that of the Zuni Indians.

The Indians with their symbolic use of colours to represent the elements and masks to show the spirit world come very close to the world of *The Thousand and One Nights* and to that described in some alchemical literature. All have an awareness and acceptance of the presence of great wonders and dark mysteries in the makeup of the world around them and are prepared to risk the dangers inherent in all exploration for the wonders of discovery. Butor would seem to be drawn to all three for the same reason — that they do not refuse to face the complexity of the world and that they attempt to capture its meanings by reproducing them in art form: dance, tale or experimental sequence. All seek a knowledge which is essential to their survival and all create a form by which to express the wisdom gained.

The juxtaposition of alchemy, modern literature and *The Thousand and One Nights* is rich in resonance; did the alchemists put their faith in chimeras or should the reader work with an equivalent patience and precision on the tales of *The Thousand and One Nights* in order to interpret the world described in them in a language as disguised as that of the alchemists themselves? Do the tales contain a wisdom hidden from the West? (After all, at the end of *Passage de Milan* and of *Portrait* the protagonist leaves for Egypt.) Or perhaps all literature should be analysed with an alchemist's care and then given over to the imagination, so that something new may result. The latter suggestion would seem to fit Butor's attitude in his own criti-

133

cism: *Histoire Extraordinaire, Essais sur les Essais, Les Sept Femmes de Gilbert le Mauvais* and *Rabelais*.

As we have seen previously these works join those of Butor and *The Thousand and One Nights* itself in the shared connection between literature and death. From this grows the myth of the author, already seen in Butor's earlier novels and especially in *L'Emploi du Temps* where the artist is presented in the role of Cain, he who is marked by death and yet does not die.[12]

Proust is of course concerned with the situation of the author and in *Les Sept Femmes de Gilbert le Mauvais* we find many of the elements of Butor's own fiction. Proust creates his narrator's world by moving out from the character to his room (he has seven in all including the one in which he is writing his book), from the room to the person connected with each one, the group which surrounds that person and so out into society as a whole. Just as the room opens on to the outside world so it also contains the privacy of the individual and by turning back through the books read within it provides a means of understanding the personality of the narrator. This double movement in the structure is enforced by the reference to seven gardens, some private, some public. Within these parallel worlds, so reminiscent of the structure of *Portrait de l'artiste en jeune singe* (and again of *The Thousand and One Nights* through its reference to Ruskin's work *Sesame and Lilies* — Vol. I: The King's Treasure, Vol. II: The Queen's Gardens), Marcel is searching for a woman he cannot destroy. Like Sheriar he seeks the eternally faithful, the indestructible. Thus Sheriar is metamorphosed into Proust's Barbe-Bleu who becomes Gilbert le Mauvais depicted in the stained glass window at Combray — a detail which connects him to Cain — so that each becomes a reflection of the position of the author. Scheherazade is thus displaced and becomes the work itself; the most faithful of women thus becoming the ultimate expression of the art of literature which alone can bring people back to life and save them for eternity. Revel, Delmont, Vernier, Proust, Butor and Scheherazade preserve their essential selves by being able to understand their surroundings well enough to be able to recount them to others, to extract the myths and transmit them to the society which produced them, and we remember Butor's statement about our world being formed to a large extent from what we have been told.[13] Salvation comes for the author from the ability to give coherent form to experience and for the reader from being aware of what is being shown to him. By these means alone can each protect himself from harm. He must learn the myths and taboos of his culture because they are "un peu comme le démon des *Mille et Une Nuits* enfermé dans une bouteille. On ouvre la bouteille et on aperçoit une gigantesque colonne de fumée qui sort de là; ces choses que nous voyons tous les jours, eh bien! nous ne les avons jamais vues!"[14]

Salvation through knowledge is the essence of Rabelais' work also, but he presents his quest in images of food and drink. Everyone in Rabelais' books is thirsty with a thirst that cannot be quenched, a thirst connected with food and an ultimate well-being that produces desire. (The only people who fast are members of the church, and we find again the insufficiency of religion expressed in *Passage de Milan*.) And as reading is drink for Rabelais, everyone is and should be drunk.

Pantagruel is a giant in relation to his world as a clear indication of the potential of a child, a potential which Gargantua developed as best he could in a way similar perhaps to the method used by Vernier. The idea of continuation and progress is strong in both cases as is the belief in education.

Rabelais' ideal place on earth is the Abbey of Thélème, but the supreme temple is that of the "Dive Bouteille" and the connection between the two as explained by Butor throws light on Butor's use of numbers in his work. We have noticed the frequent recurrence of three and above all of seven, particularly in the structure of *Portrait*, the presentation of the study of Proust and in that of Fourier's universe (seven notes in the musical scale, the eighth being a repetition of the first). Butor tells how important the number seven is in Mediaeval culture and how it was often divided into two groups of three and four, three often having a celestial force and thus being superior to four, the terrestrial counterpart (three theological virtues and four cardinal for example). The entrance to Thélème bears seven inscriptions, four prohibitions and three invitations to enter the abbey, but once inside everything is grouped by six. As Rabelais used roman numerals this should be considered as seven minus one, VI an incomplete VII. The six towers represent the six earthly directions — an immediate link with the cubic houses of the Zuni and the six houses of the Shalako which surrounded the house of the gods. When we remember that these houses used to have a hole in the roof, we realize that this was not only a way into the house but a way out — an opening to the sky and the seventh (spiritual) direction. Likewise Thélème is an incomplete version of the temple of the "Dive Bouteille" where everything is grouped in sevens and in

135

the centre of which takes place (in a dream) a symbolic representation of sexual fulfillment — the culmination of the desire expressed previously. As the body is for Rabelais a microcosm, all study thereof is thus study of the universe. Hence the double movement, private and social, in the work of Proust and of Butor is reaffirmed as showing parallel aspects of one situation. Janus, god of beginnings, who controlled Delmont's dream entry into Rome comes to mind. He was watching over past and future simultaneously and thus takes his place beside Saturn, time himself and god of the seventh day of the week.

Rabelais attributes the Egyptian language to Saturn, thus making it the language of time, the means used by time to express itself, therefore it must be capable of incorporating the whole of past, present and future. As Egyptian is also the language of Thoth, god of writing, and of Hermes Trimagisthus, tutelary of alchemy, we realize the power Butor is manipulating in his constant references to Egypt. The chain which begins with Samuel Léonard, Ahmed and Jean Ralon and continues through the whole work is explained as yet another image of the salvation to be found in language, which if properly used can fix experience and thus may be said to save the author from death.

Butor writes that Saturn's language is the oldest and youngest of all, the most fixed and the most flexible. He quotes Rabelais who continues to vaunt its importance by maintaining that everything was and will be invented within time:

et c'est la cause pourquoy les antiens ont appelé Saturne le Temps pere de Verité.[15] [sic]

So Minerva, goddess of wisdom, can share the seventh day of the week with Saturn — time, the father of all metals, lead, sulphur, the basis of alchemy and "l'homme de grande vieillesse" — thus giving more influence and power to the number seven, for everything under its protection can know the secrets of time and then achieve the wisdom which follows thereupon.

Hence we understand why Faust must be a musician; music must indeed be powerful, made as it is from a scale of seven notes and definite patterns in time. Likewise Fourier, by basing his world view on harmony and grouping his society on a musical structure, must perforce come close to perfection, at least symbolic perfection, in his social construct. Butor's development of Fourier's dream makes this abundantly clear, and the title chosen, *La Rose des Vents*, indicates that the system is one against which all other societies may be judged, for the whole globe lies within the scope of its measurement.

In contrast, six is the number of incomplete knowledge, of the inability to control events, of powerlessness within time. It is the number of sides on dice, themselves the very symbol of hazard, which by their cubic form remind us of the Zuni houses which no longer have an outlet to the seventh direction.

Given this interest in the importance of numbers we may expect Butor to be attracted by the very title of *1001 Nights*, where the extra one, by going beyond the round figure, suggests an infinite number of additions. In fact, Butor says in an interview with Georges Charbonnier:

Ce chiffre "mille et une" nuits, a en arabe un sens particulier. C'est l'équivalent d'un nombre infini. Le fait qu'il y ait "mille et une" nuits, c'est exactement comme si l'histoire durait indéfiniment.[16]   (*Ed. G.*)

And again in *Rabelais* he discusses the number briefly:

... un millier est facile à imaginer, c'est une évaluation globale;
mille suppose un dénombrement, mais nous pouvons nous le représenter aisément, en le considérant comme 10 x 10 x 10, c'est un chiffre rond;
mille et un est déjà plus difficile, mais sa relation avec le chiffre rond reste très simple; ...[17]

Hence we see that in the *1001 Nights* we have something a little more precise than a global evaluation, a little more difficult to imagine, offering more variety. Given the visual aspect of the figures Butor examines in Rabelais' work, it is certain that the possibility of reading 1001 in either direction is only too obvious; perhaps we have the 1, the first of all things, the self, the beginning of enumeration and so of time, standing guard over the 0, the totality from which it takes its meaning. Perhaps also as in Rabelais' work:

Nous pouvons considérer tous les nombres pairs comme femelles, tous les impairs comme mâles et surtout les impairs à partir du trois comme formés d'un corps symétrique auquel s'ajoute ou sur lequel se dresse le 1 supplémentaire.[18]

In this we can see the Sultan Sheriar, the first male number, apart from the couples, standing beside no one and the wholeness of experience — Scheherazade. And each is accompanied by his mirror image, his shade in the underworld which matches his reality.

Rabelais' use of numbers gives the key to the importance attributed to structure in Butor's work and his systems of language also clarify those used by Butor. We have seen how dead languages are used to indicate relatively inaccessible knowledge, lack of knowledge of a modern language to show alienation within a society. Faust is surrounded by a multitude of tongues; Rabelais provides Panurge with fourteen languages, some real, some imaginary, which surround French and all point towards it — he calls it "la rose des langues". To each is given a direction, so that the globe is covered by a network of geographical and historical communication. The language of the extreme west is that of the Antipodes, and that which is more central than French itself is Utopian; both are imaginary. As Michel Butor's house is called "aux Antipodes" we see the distance that he feels still exists between his own language and that of Fourier, which is clearly Utopian. Butor has not yet achieved the centre; on the other hand, from the outside he can see it very well.[19]

The step from Thélème to the temple of the "Dive Bouteille" is that of ultimate completion. Butor writes:

Nous voici donc, dans le temple de la Dive Bouteille, fictivement au centre de la terre, hiéroglyphe de cette intellectuale sphaere, le centre de laquelle est en chascun lieu de l'univers, la circonférence poinct (c'est Dieu selon la doctrine de Hermès Trismegistus), à laquelle rien ne advient, rien ne passe, rien ne déchet, tous temps sont praesens (et dont les songes ont quelque communication), après avoir échappé à un faux centre, l'île sonnante, la Rome des papes qui conserve, certes, dans sa corruption plus qu'une lueur de cette remarquable image du centre qu'était la Rome des empereurs.[20] [sic]

And we find elements and images of all Butor's writing. The step is the one signified by the philosopher's stone, by the hero's passage through the underworld, by the metamorphosis of the monkey. First it can be glimpsed in a dream and then perhaps brought into being if the aspirant has the necessary skills — those of language and of writing — for only by creating hieroglyphs can man fix his experience and step out of time, thus saving himself from death as surely as the prince in the Second Calender's tale.

Salvation can thus be achieved through skill in the use of language, if the full power of words has been realized. Throughout his career Butor has explored systematically every aspect of linguistic expression. Beginning with traditional prose and verse, he then developed the organization of his books, the aspect of each page of print. He has exploited the visual qualities of language in his own work and also in collaboration with artists, juxtaposing the effects of words and visual images. All this he has discussed thoroughly in

138

his criticism. In his radio plays he experimented with aural/oral effectiveness which then enabled him to create *Votre Faust* as a multi-level experience. His books are made up of a counter-point of words which produce visual or aural music — for indeed they are frequently based on musical forms.

However words are used they are always part of a system of communication; the author's communication to himself of his own experience (Revel and Delmont come to mind as well as Montaigne constantly reviewing his writing and Butor building a network of increasing complexity), but above all, language is a system for the transmission of experience from one generation to another (as it was to be for Vernier and Eller). Thus we return to the art of storytelling, the continuation of knowledge through the written word and the immortality it confers on the communicator and find ourselves once more with Scheherazade, she who escaped death through her tales and who offers, like Butor himself, a whole world of riches to be explored, knowledge to be gained, fantasy and dream to encourage the imagination. If the reader has learned how to profit from the possibilities within a book, if he is prepared to exploit these possibilities actively within his own situation, then a chain reaction can be established where the author provokes change in the reader who modifies his world because of his changing perceptions, and whose world then acts on the author in its turn. Then:

Tout est possible, l'utopie aura lieu, la faim, la soif auront raison de tout obstacle; hâtez vos labeurs ouvriers philosophes! Par l'intermédiaire de nos descendants nous ferons enfin ce que nous voudrons.[21]

CHAPTER VII: FOOTNOTES

[1] See also L. S. Roudiez, "Problems of point of view in the early fiction of Michel Butor," *Kentucky Romance Quarterly*, XVIII, 2 (1971).

[2] *Portrait*, p. 51: "In Egypt, Thoth, the god of writing, was often represented by a monkey."

[3] *Ibid.*, p. 11: "It was before I left for Egypt, that means it goes back a very long time, for Egypt has been like a second homeland for me, you might say I experienced a second childhood there."

[4] Fulcanelli, *Les Demeures Philosophales* (reprinted Paris: J. J. Pauvert, 1965), Vol. I, p. 201.

[5] Henry Hunwald, author of the Preface to Alexander von Bernus' *Alchemy and Medicine* (1904).

[6] Léonard in many ways seems to have been modelled on André Gide — belonging to a religious minority, influenced by North Africa, homosexual,

interested in the craft of writing, and he has a niece who is probably a bastard daughter. For further information on the possible influence of Gide on Butor see J. Walters, "Gide in the work of Butor," *Proceedings, Pacific Northwest Conference on Foreign Languages* (October 1969).

7 (Brussels 1966), p. 251.

8 Count Wedel, nephew of Prince Oettingen-Wallerstein by his marriage to Sophia, daughter of Countess Bellegarde née Princess von Oettingen.

9 "La balance des fées," *Répertoire*, pp. 61-73.

10 To be found in *Die Harburg im Ries* by Dr. Anton Diemand.

11 As discussed by J. Campbell, *The Hero with a Thousand Faces* (Princeton, 1949).

12 J. Walters, "Cain and the Wandering Jew in Butor's novels," *Cythera*, X (May 1971).

13 "Le roman comme recherche," *Répertoire*, pp. 7-11: "Recherches sur la technique du roman," *Répertoire II*, pp. 88-99.

14 "Propos sur l'écriture et la typographie," *Communication et Langages*, No. 13

13 "Le roman comme recherche," *Répertoire*, pp. 7-11; "Recherches sur la (March 1972), p. 29: "rather like the demon in the *Thousand and One Nights* shut in a bottle. You open the bottle and you see a gigantic column of smoke coming out of it; those things we see every day, well! we have never seen them."

15 *Rabelais*, p. 139: "and that is why the ancients call Saturn Time the father of truth."

16 G. Charbonnier, *Entretiens avec Michel Butor*, p. 41: "This figure 'a thousand and one' nights has a special meaning in Arabic. It is the equivalent of an infinite number. The fact that there should be 'a thousand and one nights' is as though the story lasted indefinitely."

17 *Rabelais*, p. 75: " ... a thousand is easy to imagine; it is a global estimation, a thousand supposes counting, but we can grasp it easily by thinking of it as 10 x 10 x 10, it is a round figure, a thousand and one is already more difficult, but its relation to the round figure is still very simple ... "

18 *Rabelais*, p. 81: "We can consider all even numbers as female, all the odd ones as male, and above all the odd numbers from 3 as making a symetrical body to which is added or upon which stands the extra 1."

19 "L'Espace du roman," *Répertoire II*, p. 44.

20 *Rabelais*, p. 137: "So here we are in the temple of the Divine Bottle, the fictitious centre of the earth, hieroglyph of this intellectual sphere, the centre of which is everywhere in the universe, the circumference-point (it is God according to the doctrines of Hermes Trismagisthus) to which nothing happens, nothing goes by, nothing is lost and all time is present (and with which dreams have some communication) after escaping from a false centre, the ringing island, Rome of the popes which certainly keeps in its corruption more than a glimmer of the remarkable image of the centre which was the Rome of the emperors."

21 *Ibid.*, p. 143: "Everything is possible, utopia will exist, hunger and thirst will overcome all obstacles; hurry your work you workmen-philosophers! By the intermediary of our descendants we shall at last do what we want to do."

APPENDIX I

L'Arc No. 39 — Contents

SPECTACLES

LIVRES

The conversations are held with R. Borderie and H. Ronse.

Cover: Collage by Jiri Kolár.

142

APPENDIX II

Bleston, Manchester and Liverpool

Bleston seems to be constructed from an amalgamation of features from Manchester and Liverpool, culled no doubt from memories of the two years M. Butor spent as French Assistant at the University of Manchester 1951-53. It has the same semi-circular layout as Liverpool, bounded by the Slee as Liverpool is by the Mersey. All three towns have docks and each had three railway stations; Manchester: Central, Piccadilly and Victoria; Liverpool: Central, Exchange and Lime Street. Bleston: Dudley, Hamilton and New Station. Each has a university, Bleston's is neo-gothic and so is Manchester's. Manchester and Liverpool both have museums which could fit the description given in *L'Emploi du Temps*; all are fairly usual provincial collections. As far as could be traced the Bleston tapestries do not exist.

Liverpool has two cathedrals, Roman Catholic and Anglican both constructed in the twentieth century; Manchester has a nineteenth-century Anglican one. Both Anglican buildings are in the gothic style. There is no other structural connection but the decoration of the Anglican cathedral in Liverpool bears a striking resemblance to details of both the Bleston churches. The Matthew window in the choir at Liverpool shows amongst other scenes the death of Abel, hence providing a possible source for the Cain window in Bleston Old Cathedral.

Links with Bleston New Cathedral are more obvious. The South Portal at Liverpool is decorated with figures representing the Liberal Arts and Science: architecture, painting, music, poetry, astronomy, mathematics, history, medicine, theology, philosophy and natural science. One of the porches at Bleston has the same subject for decoration (pp. 153 and 168). The interior of Bleston New Cathedral is decorated with examples of all earthly species. Liverpool is not decorated systematically in this way but amongst other carvings inside the building there may be found a shell, a butterfly and chrysalis, a phoenix, a peacock, a dove, a lion, fishes, wheat, a waterlily and an olive tree while various animals and human figures decorate the exterior of the building. Of these a salamander, a snake and an ape which accompany the figures of Chastity and Justice at Liverpool are mentioned at Bleston as well (p. 127).

Liverpool Cathedral has a fine peal of bells and so does Manchester Town Hall — link with Bleston. Bleston is attributed a history similar to Manchester's: an early settlement and then a Roman fort (Belli Civitas and Mancunium), and it is perhaps the knowledge that Manchester Cathedral stands on the site of a much older church that produced the idea of a temple of war under the Old Cathedral (p. 244). Manchester is a textile town and so continues the work of Yabal, son of Cain. Both Liverpool and Manchester have metal industries and thus a link with Tubalcain also. (Each has an active musical life too, but this is not given to Bleston.)

143

The perpetual rain to which Bleston is subject is the weather attributed to Manchester, said to be the wettest town in Britain. Both that and the greyness and dirt made a great impression on Butor and he tells G. Charbonnier how he suffered from the atmosphere in *Entretiens avec Michel Butor* pp. 96-97.

APPENDIX III

Plan of *Dialogue avec 33 Variations de Ludwig van Beethoven sur une valse de Diabelli**

The theme   Intervention I
1. Major march or Jupiter
                                       Intervention II

The winter ball:
2. introduction: frost
3. prelude to the waltz: through the windows of the room one sees a snowy landscape at night.
4. the Court waltz
                                      Intervention III

5. the burst of spray or morning star
                                      Intervention IV

The lovers' walk:
6. introduction: the thawing wind
7. prelude to the waltz: the troubled heart
8. the tender waltz
                                      Intervention V

9. Minor march or the Earth
                                      Intervention VI

The country fête:
10. introduction: two children running in the rain, Paul and Virginie.
11. prelude to the waltz: the couples are formed
12. the round waltz
                                      Intervention VII

13. Military march or Mars
                                      Intervention VIII

The storm:
14. introduction: the clouds gather
15. prelude to the hammer: dwarf march
The doors of the sun or the defeat of Jupiter by Saturn
16. the hammer
17. the anvil
                                      Intervention IX

18. prelude to the fantasia: the rainbow
                                      Intervention X

19. fantasia of rays
                                      Intervention XI

20. the moon
                                      Intervention XII

Divertissement of a summer afternoon:
21. overture: Oberon and Titania
22. prelude to the fantasia: Leporello-Bottom
23. Puck's fantasia
                                      Intervention XIII

24. the little fugue of Uranus
                                      Intervention XIV

The vine-growers' fête:
25. the copper waltz
26. prelude to the fantasia: the grape harvest
27. the vat fantasia
                                      Intervention XV

28. Phantom march or Mercury
                                      Intervention XVI

November meditation:
29. the phantom waltz
30. dreaming prelude to the fantasia
31. fantasia pathétique
32. the great fugue or Saturne
33. variation minuet

* This plan was given by H. Pousseur in "Ecoute d'un dialogue," *Musique en jeu*, No. 4 (Paris: Editions du Seuil, 1971).

Bibliography

Michel Butor's major works in order of publication:

Passage de Milan, (Paris: Editions de Minuit, 1954).

L'Emploi du temps, (Paris: Editions de Minuit, 1956).

La Modification, (Paris: Editions de Minuit, 1957).

Le Génie du Lieu, (Paris: Grasset, 1958).

Degrés, (Paris: Gallimard, 1960).

Répertoire, (Paris: Editions de Minuit, 1960).

Histoire Extraordinaire, essai sur un rêve de Baudelaire, (Paris: Gallimard, 1962).

Mobile, étude pour une représentation des Etats-Unis, (Paris: Gallimard, 1962).

Réseau Aérien, (Paris: Gallimard, 1962).

Votre Faust, fantaisie variable, genre opéra, *La Nouvelle Revue Française*, Nos. 109-10-11-12, (January, February, March and April 1962).

Description de San Marco, (Paris: Gallimard, 1963).

Illustrations, (Paris: Gallimard, 1964).

Répertoire II, (Paris: Editions de Minuit, 1964).

Jacques Hérold, (Paris: Editions G. Fall, 1964).

6 810 000 litres d'eau par seconde, (Paris: Gallimard, 1966).

Portrait de l'artiste en jeune singe, (Paris: Gallimard, 1967).

Essais sur les Essais, (Paris: Gallimard, 1968).

Répertoire III, (Paris: Editions de Minuit, 1968).

La Banlieu de l'aube à l'aurore suivi de *Mouvement brownien*, (Montpellier: Fata Morgana, 1968).

(*L'Arc* No. 39, *Butor* (1969) was organized and partly written by M. Butor.)

Illustrations II, (Paris: Gallimard, 1969).

Les Mots dans la Peinture, (Geneva: Skira, 1969).

La Rose des Vents, 32 rhumbs pour Charles Fourier, (Paris: Gallimard, 1970).

Où, Le Génie du Lieu II, (Paris: Gallimard, 1971).

Dialogue avec 33 variations de Ludwig van Beethoven sur une valse de Diabelli, (Paris: Gallimard, 1971).

Travaux d'approche, (Paris: Gallimard, 1972).

Les Sept Femmes de Gilbert le Mauvais, (Montpellier: Fata Morgana, 1972).

Petites Liturgies Intimes pour hâter l'avènement du Grand Transparent de Jacques Hérold, (Paris: Galerie de Seine, 1972).

Rabelais (with Denis Hollier), (Paris: Larousse, 1972).

Illustrations III, (Paris: Gallimard, 1973).

Intervalle, (Paris: Gallimard, 1973).

Répertoire IV, (Paris: Editions de Minuit, 1974).

Matière de Rêves, (Paris: Gallimard, 1975).

Illustrations IV, (Paris: Gallimard, 1976).

Second sous-sol, Matière de rêves II, (Paris: Gallimard, 1976).

For further information see G. Raillard, *Butor,* (Paris: Gallimard, 1968); F. Aubral, *Michel Butor,* (Paris: Seghers, Collection "Poètes d'aujourd'hui, 1973) and M. Spencer, "Etat présent of Butor Studies," *Australian Journal of French Studies,* III (1971).

For a bibliography of restricted editions produced in collaboration see "Bibliographie Butorienne" by A-V. Aelberts and J-J Auquier in *Revue Rêvée: Le Rêve du Déménagement* by Michel Butor Vol. VII (Braine-le-Comte: Editions Lettera Amorosa, 1975).

Selected Bibliography of Critical Works

As works on the "nouveau roman" are numerous and as most of them mention M. Butor, I have included here only books with the equivalent of one chapter on his career. Only writing in English and French is listed.

*   *   *

The following are the most easily accessible and most useful at present:

Charbonnier, G., *Entretiens avec Michel Butor*, (Paris: Gallimard, 1967).

Helbo, A., *Michel Butor, vers une littérature du signe*, (Brussels: Editions Complexe 1975).

Spencer, M., *Michel Butor*, (New York: Twayne, 1973).

Sturrock, J., *The French New Novel*, (London: Oxford University Press, 1969).

*Raillard, G., *Michel Butor*, (Paris: Gallimard, 1968).

Roudaut, J., *Michel Butor ou le livre futur*, (Paris: Gallimard, 1964).

*   *   *

Albérès, R. M., *Michel Butor*, (Paris, Editions Universitaires, 1964). "Michel Butor ou le roman transcendental," *Revue de Paris*, LXXI (1964).

Ames, Van Meter, "Butor and the book," *Journal of Aesthetics and Art Criticism*, XXIII (1964).

Attal, J-P., "Deux détectives littéraires," *Critique*, VII (1961).

Aubery, P., "Surréalisme et littérature actuelle," *Kentucky Romance Quarterly*, XIV (1967).

*Aubral, F., *Michel Butor*, (Paris: Seghers, 1973). "Un fait d'écriture généralisé," *Butor, Colloque de Cerisy*, (Paris: 10/18, 1974).

* The major bibliographical works to date are in books marked * and also F. C. St Aubyn, *Essai de Bibliographie des Oeuvres de Michel Butor*, (Paris: Klincksieck) will prove to be of major importance.

Barthes, R., *Essais Critiques*, (Paris: Editions du Seuil, 1964).
"L'activité structuraliste," *Lettres Nouvelles*, XXXII (1963).

Bosseur, D. & J-Y., "Collaboration Butor/Pousseur," *Musique en Jeu*, No. 4 (Paris: Seuil, 1971).

Bosseur, J-Y., "Votre Faust," *Les Cahiers du Centre d'Etudes et de Recherches Marixistes* (1968).
"Butor et la musique," *Butor, Colloque de Cerisy*, (Paris: 10/18, 1974).

Bourdet, D., "Michel Butor," *Revue de Paris*, LXXII (1965).

Charney, H., "15 Place du Panthéon: la mythologie du 'vérifiable' chez M. Butor," *Symposium*, XIX (1965).
"Pourquoi le 'Nouveau Roman' policier," *French Review*, XLVII (1972).

Chapsal, M., *Les écrivains en personne*, (Paris: Grasset, 1960, and 10/18 No. 809, 1973).

Daix, P., "Avec Michel Butor," *Lettres Françaises*, No. 1037 (1964).

Dällenbach, L., *Le livre et ses miroirs dans l'oeuvre romanesque de Michel Butor*, (Paris: Archives des Lettres Modernes 135, 1972).

Deguise, P., "Michel Butor et le 'nouveau roman'," *French Review*, XXXV (1961).

Ehrmann, J., "Degrés," *French Review*, XXXV (1961).

Frazer, R., "Butor's You," *New Left Review*, No. 37 (1966).

Grant, M., "The function of myth in the novels of Michel Butor," *AUMLA*, No. 32 (1969).

Greidanus, T., "L'image poétique de Butor dans *L'Emploi du Temps*," *Neophilologus*, XLII (1958).

Grieve, J., "Rencontre ou piège: a footnote to *La Modification*," *Australian Journal of French Studies*, VIII (1971).

Guyard, M-F., "Michel Butor," *Etudes*, CCXCVIII (1958).

Heppenstall, R., "The novels of Michel Butor," *The London Magazine*, II (1962).

Jaeger, P. J., "Three authors in search of an illusive reality," *Critique*, VI (1963).

Jean, R., "Degrés," *Cahiers du Sud*, LIV (1960).

Kolbert, J., "Points of view in Michel Butor's criticism: Geometry and Optics," *Kentucky Romance Quarterly*, XVIII (1971).

Lebeau, J., "De *La Modification* à *La Princess de Cleves*," *Romanic Review*, LV (1964).

Leenhardt, J., "Butor Lu," *Butor, Colloque de Cerisy* (Paris: 10/18, 1974).

Leiris, M., "Le réalisme mythologique de Michel Butor," *Critique*, XIV (1968).

Lesage, L., *The French New Novel*, (Pennsylvania State University Press, 1962).
"Michel Butor: Techniques of the Marvelous," *L'Esprit Createur*, VI (1966).

Levitt, M. P., "Michel Butor: Polyphony or the Voyage of Discovery," *Critique*, XIV (1972).

Loranquin, Al, "Michel Butor: *Degrés*," *Bulletin des Lettres* (15th March 1960).

Lydon, M., "Sibylline Imagery in Butor's *La Modification*," *Modern Language Review*, LXVII (1972).

Lyotard, J. F., *Discours et Figure*, (Paris: Klincksieck, 1971).
"La perversion du livre," *Butor, Colloque de Cerisy*, (Paris: 10/18, 1974).

Mannoni, O., "Le malentendu universel," *Les Temps Modernes*, CXXXVIII (1961).

Mansuy, M., ed., *Positions et oppositions sur le roman contemporain*, Actes et Colloques 8, (Paris: Klincksieck, 1971).

Markow-Totevy, G., "Michel Butor," *Bucknell Review*, X (1962).

Matignon, R., "Michel Butor ou la littérature menacée," *Mercure de France*, CCCLII (1964).

Matthews, J. H., "Un Nouveau Roman? Michel Butor: l'alchimie et le roman," *Situations*, No. 3 (1964).

Montal, R., "La Modification," *Le Thyrse* (1958).

Morrissette, B., "Narrative 'You' in contemporary literature," *Comparative Literature Studies*, II (1965).

Nathan, M., "Michel Butor ou un roman expérimental," *Critique*, XIII (1957).

Ouellet, R., ed., *Les Critiques de Notre Temps et le Nouveau Roman*, (Paris: Garnier, 1972).

Peillard, L., "Léonce Peillard s'entretient avec Michel Butor," *Biblio*, XXX (1962).

Picon, G., "La Modification," *L'Usage de la lecture*, II (Paris, 1961).

Pingaud, B., "Je vous il," *Esprit*, CCLXIII (1958).
Ecrivains d'aujourd'hui, (Paris: Grasset, 1960).

Pouillon, J., "Les règles du 'Je'," *Les Temps Modernes*, CXXXIV (1957).

Pousseur, H., "Ecoute d'un dialogue," *Musique en Jeu*, No. 4 (Paris: Seuil, 1971).

Puputti, L., "Le démonstratif signe de la prise de conscience dans *La Modification* de Michel Butor," *Neuphilologische Mitteilungen*, LXVII (1966).

Raillard, G., "De quelques éléments baroques dans le roman de Michel Butor," *Cahiers de l'Association Internationale des Etudes Françaises*, No. 14 (1962).

"Michel Butor notre contemporain," *Biblio*, XXXI (1963).

"Butor et la littérature," *Le Français dans le monde*, XXVIII (1964).

"Quelques notes prises au cours d'un premier déchiffrement de Michel Butor, *Où*, Le Génie du Lieu 2," *Marche Romane*, XXI (1971).

"Référence plastique et discours littéraire chez Michel Butor," *Nouveau Roman: hier, aujourd'hui*, (Paris: 10/18, 1972).

"Le butor étoilé ATTENTION," *Butor, Colloque de Cerisy* (Paris: 10/18, 1974). Raillard is the editor of this volume.

Recht, R., "Le point privilégié," *Nouvelle Revue Française*, XXVI (1964).

Ricardou, J., *Problèmes du nouveau roman*, (Paris: Seuil, 1967). ed., *Nouveau Roman: hier, aujourd'hui* (2 vol.) (Paris: 10/18, 1972).

Roelens, R., "Une recherche psychologique méconnu: le courant 'dramatique' de Georges Politzer à aujourd'hui," *La Pensée*, CIII (1962).

Roudaut, J., "Michel Butor Critique," *Critique*, VI (1960).

"Mallarmé et Butor," *Cahiers du Sud*, LVIII (1964).

"Parenthèse sur la place occupée par l'étude intitulée *6 810 000 litres d'eau par seconde* parmi les autres oeuvres de Michel Butor," *Nouvelle Revue Française*, XXVIII (1966).

"Répétition et modification dans deux romans de Michel Butor," *Saggi et ricerche di letteratura francese*, VIII (1967).

Roudiez, L. S., *Michel Butor*, (New York: Columbia Essays on Modern Writers, 1965).

"The Embattled Myths," *Hereditas* (Austin, Texas, 1965).

"Problems of point of view in the early fiction of Michel Butor," *Kentucky Romance Quarterly*, XVIII (1971).

"Aspects de la production du sens dans *Où*," *Butor, Colloque de Cerisy*, (Paris: 10/18, 1974).

French Fiction Today, (Rutgers University Press, 1972).

"Gloses sur les premières pages de *Mobile* de Michel Butor," *Modern Language Notes*, LXXXVII (1972).

"*Illustrations* — Michel Butor's criticism illustrated," *Books Abroad*, LVII (1973).

Rousseaux, A., "L'intelligence de Michel Butor," *Figaro Littéraire* (23rd Jan. 1960).

St. Aubyn, F. C., "Entretien avec Michel Butor," *French Review*, XXXVI (1962).

"Michel Butor and phenomenological realism," *Studi Francesi*, VI (1962).

"Michel Butor's America," *Kentucky Foreign Language Quarterly*, XI (1964).

"A propos de *Mobile*: Deuxième entretien avec Michel Butor," *French Review*, XXXVIII (1965).

"Butor et le Bouddhisme: l'exemple de 'Dans les flammes'," *Butor, Colloque le Cerisy* (Paris: 10/18, 1974).

Sanguineti, E., "Butor 'une machine mentale'," *Il Verri*, III (1969).

Seylaz, J-L., "La tentative romanesque de Michel Butor de *L'Emploi du Temps* à *Degrés*," *Etudes des Lettres*, III, série 2 (1960).

Simon, J. K., "A view from the train: Butor, Gide, Larbaud," *French Review*, XXXVI (1962).

"Perception and metaphor in the 'new novel'," *Triquarterly*, No. 4 (1965).

Spencer, M., "Architecture and poetry in *Réseau Aérien*," *Modern Language Review*, LXIII (1968).

"Son et lumière at the Niagara Falls," *Australian Journal of French Studies*, VI (1969).

"The unfinished cathedral: Michel Butor's *l'Emploi du Temps*," *Essays in French Literature*, No. 6 (1969).

"Michel Butor: Literature in an electronic Age," *Meanjin Quarterly*, XXVIII (1969).

"Butor et Fourier," *Butor, Colloque de Cerisy* (Paris 10/18, 1974).

Spitzer, L., "Quelques aspects de la technique des romans de Michel Butor," *Archivum Linguisticum*, XIII (1961).

Steens, M. J., "La vision chez Michel Butor," *Neophilologus*, LIII (1969).

"Le grand schism de Michel Butor," *Revue des Sciences Humaines*, XXXIV (1969).

Thody, P., "Michel Butor: la rectification," *Situations*, No. 3 (1964).

Van Rossum-Guyon, F., *Critique du Roman*, (Paris: Gallimard, 1970).

"Michel Butor, le roman comme instrument de connaissance," *Positions et oppositions sur le roman contemporain*, (Paris: Klincksiek, 1971).

"Aventures de la citation chez Michel Butor," *Butor, Colloque de Cerisy* (Paris: 10/18 1974).

Walters, J. R. Waelti-, *Alchimie et Littérature*, (Paris: Denoël, Dossiers des Lettres Nouvelles, 1975).

"Symbolism in *Passage de Milan*," *French Review*, XLII (1968).

"Gide in the works of Butor," *Proceedings, Pacific Northwest Foreign Language Conference*, XXI (1970).

"Literary Alchemy: a study of *Portrait de l'artiste en jeune singe*," *Diacritics*, I (1971).

"Cain and the Wandering Jew in Butor's novels," *Cythera*, X (1971).

"La recherche géographique et historique de l'identité butorienne," *Marche Romane*, XXI (1972).

"Juxtaposed selves: Butor's multiple presentation of character," *Essays in French Literature*, No. 9 (1972).

"Butor's use of literary texts in *Degrés*," *PMLA*, LXXXVIII (1973).

"Michel Butor and the *Thousand and One Nights*," *Neophilologus*, LIX (1975).

"*Passage de Milan*: le point de départ," *Butor, Colloque de Cerisy* (Paris 10/18, 1974).

"Butor's Museums," *Contemporary Literature*, XVIII (1977).

Index

155

157